I Woke Up Naked

The raw authentic life of a single woman
"Vulnerability sets you free"

By Tara Flaherty

Prologue

The moment I realized that for a good portion of my life I've been talking about writing a book and still haven't accomplished that yet, I became obsessed with the desire and decided to take charge at fifty one and make it happen.

I had a lot written from over the years and knew I had a lot more to write about. It was definitely a process of planning and I was getting disappointed and frustrated to say the least.

If you tell your family that you want to abruptly change your life and sell your house to write a book because you think you need to live somewhere else to make it happen can cause all kinds of havoc!

I laugh about it now because I know everyone was like, "has she lost her mind?" What can I say, I wanted to live somewhere warm all year round!

Well, maybe at fifty one we tend to get a bit off the chain while going through menopause, however I call it making sure all our boxes are checked.

I'm usually 90% positive with my life until it comes to making sure I get to live for my passions and not allow other people to interfere with it. That makes me a bit crazy and not so patient at times.

Usually when I want something to happen in my life there is a definite unstoppable passion and persistence that does not hold me back.

I planned a sabbatical party for myself and one of my friends said "so you're really going to do it?" I said, "yes, I sure am!"

My other dear friend told me she felt as if there was always something I've been searching for in my life, perhaps some peace.

This is going to take a lot of discipline because I'm not going anywhere to write this book. I'm writing in my basement sanctuary that I created for myself and I'm staying home. I told my friends and family that I won't be doing much during the next three months except working on clients and writing my book.

In January I'm going away to somewhere warm with my dog for the whole month to finish it!

If you know me then you also know how extremely busy I am with work and always entertaining someone while trying to find some time alone.

My single life is not boring at all to say the least. I have a difficult time putting my needs in front of others, however I'm very aware of it and feel a desire to learn how to do that with no guilt.

I am excited and ready to indulge in this writing to help inspire people from all over the world to follow through with whatever your hopes and dreams may be.

To squash your fears and start living the life you desire.

I woke up naked many times in my life feeling very vulnerable to what lies ahead. It's a mindset that you have to be fully aware of and want to live a great life.

As you read my book you will see all the life altering situations I've been through with my personal, professional and love life. However, I have put a positive spin on it and refuse to live unhappily. Waking up unhappy and not having the capability to change it is one of my biggest fears.

When we stay in our past we cannot have a healthy vision of our future.

I would love for my book to be a number one seller and I would love to meet Steve Harvey someday!

My intention is that my book will be as good as his "Act Like a Lady, Think Like a Man." If you ever want someone to motivate you, listen to his podcasts. He will inspire you all day long!

I'm not an expert on much, however there are a few things I'm pretty good at. Independence, perseverance, vulnerability and being single.

Being good at being single doesn't mean you can't date someone or have a partner, it means you can solely take care of yourself in every aspect while living alone.

I also like to think I'm pretty creative as well.

This book is designed to be about the raw authentic life of a single woman, "I Woke Up Naked" means vulnerability.

I've been single a good portion of my life so I have a lot to say and want to encourage people to be OK while living alone and to not feel ashamed, scared, judged or intimidated by society that thinks there's something wrong with you.

I'm not saying that I encourage divorce or splitting up, I'm saying if you have exhausted all of your resources in fixing the marriage/relationship and you're still miserable then it is OK to value yourself and move forward to a happy life.

People are single for all kinds of reasons such as they haven't found the right one, divorce, widowed or they didn't want a divorce but their spouse did.

It's OK and you will feel naked and lost at first, however if you don't hold onto any regrets, vengeance or feelings of low self worth then I promise you will find yourself and live your best life.

It's a choice.

I love love, I'm just not an expert on that when it comes to relationships but who the hell is?

A few years ago I became ordained so that I could marry my friends and now I have married seven couples. I feel blessed that people trust me to deliver such a sacred vow to each other.

What an honor!

In the first several chapters I'm going to talk about my life leading up to this point so you can relate to why and what brought on my extreme independence in my journey throughout my life.

I hope you can relate to them and some of my stories are inspiring as well.

Over the past several years I have been reading inspirational books that have helped me grow internally as well as understand that all that I have desired in my life I was perhaps creating through the Secret, the Law of Attraction. I have been manifesting my life and I didn't even know it.

My daughter recently told me I was the master of manifesting!

The hardest part of this mindset is feeling as if you already have it. I must fall short with that part a little or I would be rich and madly in love with the man of my dreams!

But let's not get negative...... That's coming for me.

Who says you can't have it all?

OUTLINE

1. My journey through childhood
A. Life on the farm
B. Heart broken
C. Blended Family
D. New life in the city
E. Home sweet home

2. My journey into adulthood
A. Life changing moment
B. A mothers trust
C. Another love
D. Becoming extremely brave
E. Taking a risk
F. Dreadful fire
G. Our dream home
H. It's a chain
I. Broken heart again
J. Wilted plant dying of thirst (my perception of marriage)
K. Feeling freedom

3. My journey into singlehood
A. New relationships and friendships
B. Charlie
C. Who am I
D. Feeling unconditional love (Pablo)
E. Loving myself

4. Beyond success
A. To Find your purpose
B. To create
C. To find your resources
D. To have faith
E. Motivation
F. Positive mental attitude
G. Enthusiasm
H. Concentrate
I. Receptive
J. Team player
K. Resilience
L. Serve-go above and beyond
M. Discipline
N. Balance

5. My Journey into true vulnerability
A. Just a girl and her dog
B. Discovery of my journey
C. Acknowledgments
D. Testimonials
E. About the author

My journey through childhood

Life on the farm

As we drove up a long lane I could see a big white house that appeared very old. It was the creepiest house with a huge barn on the hill. It looked as though it had been abandoned. We were meeting someone there but I wasn't sure why.

We got out of the car and started looking around, as we entered the front of the house we could smell something so gross. The inside of the house was so disgusting I think they must've had several animals living there.

My sisters Lori, Heidi and I asked, "why are we here?" Mom said, "this is going to be our new home." What?? We started to cry and said, "we're going to live here? No way, we don't want to live in this dump!"

Mom and Dad started to laugh and assured us that they could fix it up and it would be beautiful. We would be in the country and have lots of animals and woods to play in so we were not to worry.

It took several months of working day and night but it was beautiful when it was done. Mom could do anything. She was the wallpaper queen! She taught us how to do anything we set our minds to.

When spring came around it was also a disaster on the outside, definitely hard work fixing the barn, cleaning up the yard and putting in a huge garden.

We became ready for our new farm life. We had cows, a horse, pigs, chickens, goats, ducks, cats and dogs. Our happy family inside and out.

You learn so much living on a farm. True survival as we ate everything we raised and grew. We learned to can all kinds of vegetables and we would spend hours snapping beans. That wasn't my favorite thing to do that's for sure, however I'm blessed that my parents taught us so many valuable things.

We all sat at the dinner table every night with a full course meal, and we absolutely had better use our manners! Dad was big on that, licking our fingers was a big NO NO! I still have issues with that, I won't date a man that licks his fingers that's for sure.

I loved going on hikes in the woods with my sisters looking for mushrooms or just exploring. We weren't allowed to stay inside all day unless we were sick or it was raining.

If it was raining, Mom would try to teach us to sew. She could make anything as she made a lot of our clothes. I wish I would have wanted to learn how to sew more back then but I enjoyed being outside, perhaps bailing hay or taking care of the animals instead.

Being in tune to nature every day and learning hard work were the best values my parents could have given us, we were always grateful for what we had. If we weren't grateful there would always be a hard lesson learned from Mom!

I can remember getting woken up on the weekends to Mom playing Tammy Wynette or Loretta Lynn, it was our cue to get up and get busy doing something such as, clean the house, weed the garden, or pick up sticks so Dad could mow the yard. We had to help with most everything.

Growing up in the seventies was by far nothing like it is today. Playing video games was not an option. I don't even think we had any such thing. All I can remember is playing Pac Man on an occasional machine I came across maybe at the fair or something like that and I definitely was not good at all.

We rode our bikes on country roads trying to avoid dogs that just came running after us. We feared for our lives but we did it anyway! We knew that if we wanted to get to the other side we better pedal as fast as we could so we could get to the lake.

We had to use our imagination for entertainment because we only had one black and white tv with NO remote control! Little House on the Prairie was our choice tv show everyday, however when it was over we had better get busy filling the wood box as a wood burner was our source of heat.

If we wanted to hang out with our friends we had to walk or ride our bikes to their house to find out what they were up to and that would usually consist of us all rallying up for a good kickball or softball game. We drank water out of the garden hose if we were thirsty and at times we would be gone for hours and our parents did not even miss us unless we weren't home by dark.

One time my sisters and I ran away into the cornfield because we overheard our dad saying he was going to drown some kittens in the pond because we had so many strays running around. We were gone for hours and they didn't even notice, however we did save the kittens! Dad would have never done something like that but we believed him back then.

Our entertainment was also with our animals. We had pigs and we would hang on to their tails while they took us for a ride through the mudd and, YES through shit as well! Our hefer, Bess, took us for a ride through the pastures and thank god she wasn't a bronking bull. We did have one bull but couldn't find a way to successfully break him.

We had a huge palomino horse named Sheba. We couldn't get up on her back so she would put her head down and we would sit on her neck and she would lift us up onto her back. We rode her bareback most of the time. We had a lot of trails to ride her through the woods that lead us to a big open field. She would take us on the ride of our life. That was so fun!

The worst part about being a farm girl was getting attached to the animals. I had a cow named Eddie, he was my pet and every day I couldn't wait to see him and take care of him. One day I came home from school, went to the barn to see him and he was gone. I asked Dad where he was, he just looked at me with glossy eyes and said, "we couldn't afford to feed him anymore, times were tough!"

I cried, I cried so hard! I refused to eat red meat for a month for fear I would be eating my precious pet Eddie. That was the first time I was ever allowed to say when I WASN'T going to eat something! I didn't speak to my dad for a couple weeks. Now that I am an adult I understand but boy I didn't back then. Let's just say having a dog as a pet is a much better choice than a farm animal. They each have a purpose.

I have to say being raised on a farm was truly my best life memory. Finding this run down sixty acre farm was a big risk to take on, however it was the best thing to teach my sisters and I, to not be afraid to turn something so horrible into something beautiful!

Most anything can be rescued if you have a vision and put in the work.

We are all three fearless women when it comes to a rehab project. I think we are all so fearless now that it even scares Mom sometimes! We've all taken on some pretty challenging projects.

"If you believe, you can achieve."

As my sisters and I grew older we became very active in sports. I was a cheerleader, played softball and ran track. We lived several miles from the school so Mom got tired of the constant drive and was ready to move to town.

Dad loved the farm but lost the battle to us girls.

We were his world back then....

Heartbroken

We bought a cool brick house right in town with a big front porch. It was another rehab. Once again Mom and Dad turned it into a beautiful home for us. I wanted my room decorated in rainbows. I always loved to see a rainbow and I wanted my room to be happy.

We loved hanging out on the porch with our friends. We became the "Burkepile sisters". It didn't take long to get ourselves into trouble having friends over when we weren't supposed to or going to our friends house having boys over when we weren't allowed.

My sister Heidi and I decided to sneak out one night to go to a boys campout. We locked the bedroom door and put pillows under the sheets to look like we were in the bed. We climbed out of the window onto the roof and jumped down on the ground. Big dumb dumbs! We made it to the camp out but got caught because we locked the stupid door. Definitely got whipped with a belt for that one!

We missed the farm life but living in town was the start of a new chapter in our lives. My sisters and I adjusted well, however I'm not so sure my parents did. I feel like they were growing apart, not really living for us anymore because they were working a lot and not spending much time together.

Mom got a job at the local marina where she met some new friends and Dad was a semi truck driver so there wasn't a lot of time for each other.

My sisters and I stayed busy with our sports and friends but not really much family time anymore. **Nothing like we had living on the farm.**

After living in town for about a year my mom wanted to go on vacation with just my dad. I think she was trying to get their spark back from all the adjustments they had been adapting to. He declined so she went by herself. He didn't like to do much besides work a lot.

I'm sure Dad always felt a lot of regret from that and wished he would have been more vulnerable to my moms aspirations.

Your life can turn into a different direction at any given moment, for better or worse.

**The lesson of closed doors
Is to do better next time.
The lesson of open doors is
To do something NOW.** -Daniel Pink-

As I walked home from school, I wondered if I would ever see her again. I know she loved us but I also know she wasn't happy and the feeling of, "what if she doesn't come back", was clearly in my mind…

I remember standing in the kitchen when the phone rang and it was her. I was so excited to hear from her, I missed her so much because it had been nearly one month since I last saw her. We talked for a while and she sounded sad, she asked to speak to Dad. I stayed on the other line and heard her tell him that, "she wasn't coming home", I hung up the phone and just started sobbing!

They say that nothing happens overnight, well that was one life-changing moment….

The feeling I had that afternoon was exactly true, my MOM wasn't coming home! I was devastated but all along I could feel it in my heart. I was angry, hurt, and scared because Mom was always there for us and now she was miles away. We had rocky times as a family but we always had a good solid home.

Mom and Dad were wonderful parents who lived their lives for my sisters and I. We didn't have a lot growing up but I have fond memories of my childhood and never remember going without the necessities of life. We didn't get a lot of toys but what we had we really enjoyed.

However, there was a time that we were at the Benjamin Franklin store in my hometown and I was probably seven years old at the time. I asked my mom for a playwatch and some old maid cards. She told me "no". Well apparently I didn't like being told "no", so I took them anyway. Yes, I became a little thief!

Months later, my sis Heidi and I were playing with our plastic farmyard toy set, that's where I had the items hidden so she found them. I begged her not to tell Mom! She didn't want me to be a little thief so she told on me and I got the whipping of a lifetime!

They taught us to work hard for what you have, be good and honest and life will be good to you.

My Mom was a daughter of eleven children and my Dad was a son of seven. They were also taught to work hard, act right or else and didn't have a lot growing up. My mom didn't even have running water in the house.

My grandpa had disowned my mom at seventeen because she was pregnant with my oldest sister.

He wanted nothing to do with her and he didn't show up for her wedding. That hurt my mom for many years.

He finally came around after my sister was born and fell in love with her. He died a few years later in a bad accident while getting hit in his car by a semi truck driver. How devastating! I'm pretty sure she was pregnant with me when that happened.

Then my grandma had a stroke several years later. It was a massive stroke that she had to learn how to walk and talk all over again. Mom also lost her oldest sister while giving birth to her niece because she had a blood clot in her leg that went to her lung.

When I was seven, Mom lost my baby sister at full term from the umbilical cord being wrapped around her neck. I remember it like it was yesterday....

My sisters and I were staying at my grandparents that night patiently waiting for my dad to bring us the news. We were in bed and I can remember my dad coming upstairs to tell us that our baby sister died. We all just cried with our dad hugging him so tight. They really struggled from losing their baby.

I can't even imagine my mom going through all of that at such young stages of her life. So many tragic things that I'm sure were difficult for her to heal from.

My parents were wonderful people that just got married young but stayed committed for the sake of us girls.

It was going to be a terrible adjustment without having my mom around.

Sometimes having too much freedom can be a disaster, and that's exactly what it was...

It was the summer of my eighth grade year and we all got through the many sad days of Mom being gone.

My oldest sister Lori became the rock of our family, she was so strong, she always was the mothering type. I have to say that her and her boyfriend at the time were our saviors. Mom sure did teach her how to take charge of a situation!

Dad became a heavy drinker, he passed out every night and I, at thirteen, decided to try out that part as well.

One night my sisters came home to find me throwing up and choking in my sleep from drinking too much Canadian Whiskey. They had to help me and put me in the shower. The scary thing is, I don't even remember that and apparently it traumatized my sisters enough to say, "I should be grateful to be alive!"

Not only did I start drinking, but smoking became somewhat of a habit as well. I didn't care about anything anymore. I was a cheerleader so doing these bad things were totally out of character for me.

Even though my personality was feisty, spontaneous, and fun loving it was not like me to become so weak.

As I look back now, that saying "you have to find your weaknesses so that your strengths can overcome them!"

Believe me… it didn't take long to figure that out!

Blended Family

Dad had finally stopped crying and decided it was time to start dating....

Well, I think my sisters and I got used to the idea of it just being us and our dad, perhaps we weren't ready for someone to take Mom's place yet.

He came home one day with one of Mom's friends. We liked her a lot when she was Mom's friend but we weren't so sure we wanted her to date Dad. She was very nice to us but we weren't ready to have another woman in the house, interfering with the possibility of Mom coming back. We were not very nice to her at all!

I feel bad about that sometimes because I have to wonder how our lives would've been if we hadn't ran her off. After that, we decided we had to let dad do as he wished.

So one day he brought another friend of my mom's home. She was a friend of my mom and dad's for a long time. They were best friends so we knew her since we were born. She had a son and a daughter, she was so cute. I became very attached to the girl because I had always wanted a little sister. She was around the same age as my little sister Katie

Marie who died at birth when I was seven years old. I was heartbroken over that so I was happy to have her around.

We really enjoyed Dad dating this lady, we had always liked her a lot. She even tried to go back to her second ex-husband that abused her so we cried and begged her not to go. She came to her senses and stayed with Dad and we became very close to her.

I always missed my mom, but it was nice to have someone to spend time with, we felt like maybe we could be happy again.

Mom had asked us to move with her when she left but we all wanted to stay with Dad because we had our life here with our friends and we couldn't imagine moving away. I'm sure that it was hard for my mom to adjust to not having her girls with her.

During this time my grandma and grandpa decided to put their farm up for sale and move to Tennessee. It was the farm where my dad grew up so he really wanted to buy it and move there. He was so happy because he hated living in town. We were excited because we liked living on a farm, however we enjoyed living in town as well.

We all moved in together and it was so much fun at first but then reality kicked in for everyone….

I started to really miss my mom and this other woman became very hard to live with, however I'm sure dealing with three teenage girls was not easy as well.

She became so different that it seemed as though she didn't like us anymore. We couldn't do anything right and we started feeling like strangers in our own home. This home we felt safe in was no longer for us, it was all about her and her daughter.

Every day there was a new rule in the house. It was like she had become a different person and Dad was still drinking heavily so he didn't notice nor would he do anything about it.

My dad's parents divorced when he was a teenager so when my grandpa got remarried that's when my dad was taught the importance of standing by his woman, however at least my step grandma was a nice person.

My sisters and I were definitely being shoved aside and her daughter was clearly the only one who mattered anymore.

We had to strip our clothes off before coming into the house after riding our horses, we had to be careful with everything we touched before washing our hands.

She would watch us like a hawk about washing our hands. She was obsessed about it! She would even listen outside the bathroom door to make sure we would wash them like we were some sort of filthy creatures or something. As if my mom and dad hadn't taught us to be mindful of that! It was a sanitary obsession.

Meanwhile, she would have twelve cats living in the house along with baby chickens and rarely cleaned the house thoroughly. That made no sense!

She made us wrap our sanitary items in a newspaper for fear we would use too much toilet paper. We had to use old raggy towels for showering and oh my goodness we had to clean and dry out the shower every single time! Every inch or else!!! It was so clear what was happening.

I remember her writing notes on everything with masking tape saying "don't touch, don't eat", it was for her daughter.

She had a big black garbage bag locked in her bedroom full of good food like captain crunch and hohos for her daughter and we were left with raisin bran and ginger snaps!

I guess it was no longer my dad's money to buy groceries, it was hers. She didn't even work that much. She drank wine coolers a lot while sunbathing.

She had a book of rules for us that was nine pages long. I could keep rambling on but you get my point? Prime example of a wicked, hopefully not step-mother treating us as if we are not worthy.

She called us brats one time and even spelled it out for us **B-R-A-T-S!** I wanted to tell her that I almost won the spelling bee several times so I know how to spell but that would be pushing my luck as being disrespectful. I can be a bit of a smart ass at times!

Well she got her way, Lori moved into town with my grandma and I moved to Arlington, Virginia with my mom. Heidi stayed for a year longer than us but I know it wasn't pleasant for her. I'm sure my dad was hurt, but I couldn't live like that and he had forgotten who his family was.

That's how he was when it came to making hard decisions. He didn't like conflict. I'm sure that was another reason my mom left. She had to make all the decisions and be the disciplinarian with us girls. If he were to wip us he would say, "act likes this hurts"! It would definitely hurt him more than it would us.

I was so sad because I loved my family and my friends. I didn't want to leave them but I was so unhappy and I needed to feel loved again.

My mom made me feel safe and I missed her so much. So I packed my things, said my goodbyes, and was off to a new life with my mom and her new family.

When you blend families or if you become a step parent it's so important to treat all the children equally. Really doesn't matter what age they all are. It's very hurtful and could definitely cause self worth issues!

I was the youngest child and couldn't say that I was a daddy or mommy's girl. I feel as if I was both. I loved them so much and was equally bonded to both of them. I was sick a lot as a child with terrible ear infections and allergies so I imagine that is why I always got a lot of attention as well. My sisters would call it SPOILED, however I was extremely sad when we all parted ways as a family.

I would like to share some poems I wrote for my mom and dad during this time. I believe I was thirteen or fourteen when I wrote them.

Mom and Me

Mom and me are two of a kind
We stick together
Most of the time.
I love you mom
With all my heart,
I know forever
We'll never part.
Even though
We are miles away,
I still think of you
Day after day.
I think what is
Meant to be,
Love and friendship
Mom and me.

"There's no way to be a perfect mother, And a million ways to be a good one."

-Jill Churchill-

My dearest Dad

The times that we have spent
Are precious to me
I love you dearly Dad,
I hope that you can see.
You mean the world to me
In every special way,
The wonderful things you do
Make me joyful everyday.
There's times I can't express
The love I have for you
You are the greatest Dad
I'll love you each day through.

"I cannot think of any need in Childhood as strong as the need for a father's protection."

-Sigmund Freud-

New life in the city

As we drove into the big city I became very anxious and excited to be going to my new home. It was kind of scary because I was used to living in a small town with only one traffic light and I knew everyone, well almost everyone.

Now I'm going to live in this big city that is fifteen minutes from Washington, DC and I didnt even know a soul, not even my new family really.

Mom married a man who was an officer in the Marine Corps, she met him in Maine while she was on vacation. He was a very tall man with dark hair and appeared to be very worldly. I'm assuming that's why my mom was attracted to him. He was a take charge kind of person and wanted to show my mom the world. He had two children, Tara who was my age and Sean who was eight.

My new home was in an apartment complex with only two bedrooms, one bathroom, a very small kitchen, dining room and a living room. It had a pool right outside our back door.

Tara and Sean were visiting for the summer but once we all met they decided they would like to live there as well.

We had a lot of fun and met all kinds of friends from the complex.

It was a very tight living situation so we had to find a bigger apartment within the complex with three bedrooms and a much larger living area. I had to share a bedroom with Tara, I've always had my own room so it was going to be an adjustment.

Even though I was living with my mom now and felt very safe and loved, I started to miss the rest of my family. It was so hard because when I was with one I would always miss the other. I had never been away from my sisters and we were always so close. They were my best friends.

Tara, Sean and I got along well because they were facing the same feelings. They moved there from Florida and although they had their dad and each other they still missed their mom and friends as well. Their mom and dad had been divorced for a while but they still had to start a new life just like I did.

It was time for school to start and I was going to a new high school into the ninth grade. I tried not to seem scared but it was so overwhelming because where I came from the school was so small and all the kids were of the same race. My new school there were kids from all over the world. There were white, black, Polish, Hispanic, Chinese, Japanese and many more. The school was so huge there were probably 2500 students. My old school had approximately 450. How could a girl not be scared?

I have never been a person to be scared of people but this time it was different, I tried not to act like it but I was very intimidated on the inside.

Tara and I had some classes together so we looked out for each other. I worried about her because she was kind of backwards and wasn't as outgoing as I was. I was the rebel and she was the good girl. She was cool though, we helped each other in different ways. She was Booksmart and I was possibly more people smart. She helped me with my homework and I helped her look and feel better about herself.

We both made friends and got involved in school activities. I made the varsity softball team and she joined the band.

Things were going well until I started hanging out with the more rebellious crowd. I guess I was attracted to that because I was so adventurous, love taking risks and having fun. I became grounded three weeks out of every month because the week I wasn't grounded I would get myself into trouble again.

What a challenge I had become. I would skip school, get drunk, smoke cigarettes, and lie about where I was going and go to the nearest party. That year was probably the worst year.

Just recently, I told my mom about me skipping school one day with some kids and we went on the subway to Crystal City underground mall. She couldn't believe it, I was fourteen and wasn't even scared.

I guess I just didn't care about much anymore. I seemed happy on the outside but on the inside I felt like I was dying.

There was a time when I felt like life wasn't worth living anymore. Even though I was living like a normal teenager my emotions were getting the best of me. I was trying to adjust to all of these changes in my life but inside I was so homesick and distraught. I felt like no matter where I was living I was always homesick for someone.

<u>I especially missed our happy home.</u>

One night without ever noticing that I was having these thoughts I took twenty four sudafed pills because I decided I didn't want to live anymore. If my family couldn't be together then I would just take the pain away. It was a feeling that is hard to describe.

You feel so helpless and full of despair. I felt like nothing would ever be the same again, perhaps not capable of really understanding that life is full of changes and possible heartaches.

Little did I know that sudafed was for a cold and not really a harsh drug. So of course I woke up the next morning feeling better than ever. My sinuses were clear and I was so truly happy to be alive!

How devastated my parents would've been and how selfish and weak I was to think that life was all about me.

After that day I think I was meant to live this life in full force! I'm sure I still gave my parents trouble but I gained strength to help me through my troubled times. I didn't tell anyone about that until I was well into my adult years.

I would like to speak to broken families. Please pay close attention to your child during difficult

or abrupt changes especially teenagers as they may be really good at hiding pain like I was. Therapy is always good during a divorce or maybe spending time alone with that child just to keep the communication open. They need to know they are still important after a divorce no matter what age they are and still need that bonding time.

I do not judge my parents for getting a divorce, in fact, I know they really tried to make it work. I left out the fact that they divorced twice. They got remarried right before we bought the sixty acre farm. I don't have a good memory of that, however I'm extremely grateful they gave us those memories of living on the farm.

After a long year of adjustments that came to an end as well. My stepfather got orders to move to Jacksonville, North Carolina. Once again, we were moving to a new home and school. We all stayed together, this time my sister Heidi was also moving with us. I was so excited because I missed her so much.

My mom and stepfather bought a house with four bedrooms. This time Heidi and I shared a bedroom. We lived within walking distance from the school, the neighborhood had lots of kids our age so it didn't take long to meet new friends. We also lived pretty close to the ocean so I loved that.

The school was a lot smaller than Virginia so it wasn't as intimidating on the first day. We all fit in pretty well, that was the good thing about moving so much because it became easier meeting new people and making new friends. I truly love people and always try to see good in them before I see bad. I like being this way, sometimes I get hurt but that's life. I would never want to be any different.

I got a job in the mall at a little place called Cookie Kitchen. Every time I worked I got asked out or received a present from a different Marine. Camp Lejeune was stationed in Jacksonville, NC. There were good looking Marines everywhere you went. If only I weren't so young! I looked older as a teenager than I actually was so that's probably why, however I would always decline the dates. Big dumb dumb!

It was fun working there, however if I was ever going to be overweight it would have been then. The cookies were delicious!

I made a lot of great friends. I Played softball and was in the school newspaper class.

I had played softball my entire life so I like to think I was pretty good. I was the varsity backup pitcher my freshman year in Virginia and I was pretty proud of that. Fastpitch was my thing, however in North Carolina it was slowpitch. I had to learn all the new rules of the game. The batting is so different and you couldn't steal the bases so I struggled with that for sure.

I was fast and fearless back then!

I loved living in North Carolina, however I was always missing my friends and family in Ohio. That feeling never went away for me. I felt safe living with my mom but my heart was also in Ohio.

I became stronger and wasn't getting into as much trouble anymore. Maybe I was getting smarter at hiding it because I still drank, smoked and skipped school occasionally or perhaps I was attracting different types of friendship. Possibly friends that my mom liked and trusted as well.

Saying goodbye was always going to be hard to do no matter where I decided to live…..

Home sweet Home

It was during the middle of my junior year that my sister Heidi and I decided to move back to Ohio. We had made some great friends, but we still longed for our hometown friends and family.

A lot happened through the years but I felt like enough time had passed that I could move back home with my dad, so I gave it a second chance.

He got married to this woman while I was gone so I thought maybe things would be better….

Well, I guess the couple of years wasn't long enough because it still wasn't a safe, loving place. My dad still could not mold us together as a family. I know it was hard for him but the outcome needed to be up to him and he couldn't understand what was really happening nor did he try.

My parents had different rules for me after the divorce.

My dad would let me smoke and drink because he said if you're going to do it I want you to do it in front of me!

My mom grounded me for three weeks out of every month because she said I had to wait to do bad things until I was eighteen!

My stepfather was a very strict Marine and always gave my mom a hard time about me. He didn't discipline me, however he would definitely badger my mom until I was on lock down with nothing to focus on except my homework and the four walls in my bedroom!

My stepmom didn't care, she just wanted to find fault in everything I did. She wasn't loving or supportive like a teenage girl needed in their life. She was always trying to catch me doing something wrong.

For example, I believe it was the summer I came to visit in between my freshman and sophomore year. Heidi and I were upstairs with a couple of friends getting ready to go to a dance place called night moves.

My stepmom came up and told me I was no longer allowed to smoke in the house because she thought I put my cigarettes out in a cardboard box lid. I assured her that I didn't do it! She wouldn't believe me no matter what I said she kept accusing me of it.

My temper finally came out and I called her a few names, "yes I know they were not kind." She told my dad what I said and he beat the shit out of me! My sister Heidi tried to protect me but it just became a disaster! He started banging our heads together in a hold on us so we couldn't leave!

Now, my dad rarely spanked us growing up so I don't want you to think he was an abuser by any means. He just lost his shit that day!

Our friend Heather's boyfriend came to get us and after that was when Heidi ended up moving with us to North Carolina.

We didn't speak to Dad for eight months and it was during that time they got married.

Sad thing about that story was that many years later as an adult my stepsister ended up admitting that she and her friend were the ones that put the cigarettes out in the cardboard box lid at eight years old.

I imagine that broke my dads heart but he never did say he was sorry for that nor did my stepmother. My step sister thought it was funny but I was extremely upset over it!

I moved in town with my older sister Lori to a small one bedroom apartment. She was nineteen and I was sixteen. She became a mother figure to me as well and was always my best friend.

For the most part I was pretty responsible, I loved to drink beer so that was probably the worst thing she had to put up with.

Oh… and I had a boyfriend so I'm sure that caused her a bit of stress as well. I thought I was madly in love with a farm boy. Imagine that!

I went to school every day and worked almost every night. I paid my own way as much as I could. I was a waitress so I made pretty good money.

I tried to play softball again, however after I played slow pitch I ended up losing my timing on how to hit a fastpitch ball. I would stay after practice every night in the batting cage but no matter how hard I tried I just couldn't get it back.

I was an excellent pitcher but once the coach saw how bad my batting was he never played me. I also lost my pitch. I was so disappointed in myself that I ended up quitting. I was never a quitter but I was so competitive and couldn't stand sitting on the bench. I blamed the coach for a long time for that.

However, now that I'm an adult I can see that the outcome needs to be up to me!

The next year was my senior year and I only needed one credit to graduate so I took OWE (occupational work education). I got out of school every day at 11:30.

Working a lot became a big part of my life as I needed to save money for college. I wanted to go to Ohio State School of Cosmetology and become a hairstylist. That was always a big dream of mine. Or to become a rodeo star.

Recently, I rode a mechanical bull and I was so thankful that I chose to be a hairstylist, my legs were bruised and hurt for weeks after!

I graduated from high school in 1989 with a small scholarship to the school I wanted to attend, applied for grants and a loan so that fall I was off to beauty college!

I moved into an apartment with three other girls whom I'd never met before because it was an hour away from my hometown.

We did pretty well living together at first. I was hardly ever there because we went to school forty hours a week and then I had to work thirty hours after that to pay for all my living expenses. Going to school and work had become a habit for me so it wasn't too bad.

Fast food and Ramen noodles became my regular diet. Fast food because I was too busy and Ramen noodles because I was too poor!

I ended up not getting along with one of the girls I lived with. She told some lies about me smoking Marijuana to my teacher, back then I would never ever think about doing something like that. However, some friends of mine did at a party we had one night but I would not rat on them.

Being a tattle tail was definitely not in my nature!

It luckily backfired on her and they kicked her out of the program for causing too much drama. KARMA at its finest! I really don't know what her problem was with me even to this day, as I'm usually able to get along with most everyone. Maybe that was the problem, everyone liked me but she struggled making friends.

Hopefully she has become a nicer person as an adult!

I believe there are three reasons bad things happen to you. Karma, you can't control what others do or it's just life!

I was dating my high school love at the time and he would come and stay with me on the weekend or bring me home so I didn't get too homesick. His family became my family. I would stay at his house when I went home. They made me feel welcome, loved and valued.

I worked in a restaurant in the mall when I first moved there, York Steakhouse I believe. One night my boyfriend came to pick me up on a Friday night. He was just sitting there waiting for me to get my chores done when I saw some guys running around but I just thought it was our cooks being silly and chasing each other. I looked over at my boyfriend and he was white as a ghost...

We were being robbed at gunpoint and I didn't even know it!

I had a hearing problem and the music was playing so I didn't hear anything that was happening.

Apparently the guy came in through the back door that didn't shut all the way from ice building up on it. I personally thought it was a planned inside job but we will never know. Thankfully nobody was hurt! They did catch the guy but it was kind of traumatizing for a while afterwards.

I ended up taking a job with Kids R Us. It was right behind my apartment within walking distance. I didn't have a driver's license or a car so that would be ideal for me. It also seemed a little safer for me and would put me in tune for possibly liking kids someday!

It was a long year but I did it and what an accomplishment it was for me!

I look back now and wonder if I was living my life through the secret back then.

I realized that I had to because there was no room for failure in my life.

I wanted to make my parents proud of me. I was a bad teenager so there was no way I was going to let them down as an adult.

I wanted to be a winner!

State board was a breeze and I was on my way to fulfilling my dream!

There have been many people in and out of my life that are very dear to my heart. During my times of struggle so many people came to my rescue. For several years I was lost not really having a home of my own.

I had lived with my sister, different friends and their families before I went to college and after. I was an adopted daughter and sister to many. I will never forget all those special people in my heart who had faith in me and encouraged me all the way.

Some of those people are still in my life but then there are some that are still in my heart that I don't see anymore.

I understand that there will be people that come into your life for a certain reason. It's called the law of attraction. I believe in my life, with all that I have done in every chapter, there is someone new going through it with me.

"Love as hard as you can, be grateful for what you have but attach yourself to nothing because you never know how quickly your life may change."

I'm not sure who said this quote exactly like this but I like it.

Change is perhaps the only sure thing in life.

The seasons change, weather changes, time changes and then sometimes things happen that can change your life forever….

"The greatest discovery of all time
Is that a person can change his future
By merely changing his attitude."

-Oprah Winfrey-

My journey into adulthood

My life changing moment

In 1992 my life was about to change drastically. I was dating a guy whom I'd been friends with for a long time. He was a rebound for me because I had just broken up with my high school love of four years. We had been dating for about six months, I was on birth control, however I got sick and had to be on an antibiotic and nobody ever told me that would cancel out the birth control.

At twenty years old I found out I was pregnant. It was time for a major wake up call!

I was living with my best friend at the time, we were having so much fun living our best life. We lived in a Mobile home on "Tom Dick Harry" street. Isn't that such a funny name for a street? We worked hard and played hard too. We drank a lot but we were both very responsible.

After I found out I was pregnant I got nervous that I wouldn't be able to afford to live on my own and take care of my baby. I needed to save money because I was going to be a single mom now.

I cared very much for my baby's father, however I didn't feel in love with him to stay together. I was still trying to move past my breakup with my high school love. I guess after my parents divorce, love became hard for me to hold on to or trust so easily. I was a hot mess and there is more to the story that I choose not to revisit. I did love him as a friend though.

I decided once again to make an effort to live with my dad as he was the only immediate family I had to rely on at the time.

Mom lived in North Carolina, Heidi was in the Navy and Lori lived an hour away. I had no choice but to reach out again if I wanted the comfort of family while I was about to become a single mother.

We talked about the past and worked things out as much as we could and let go of all the resentment. I forgave my dad and stepmother and they made me feel at home. It felt good to forgive them as I was about to become a parent myself. I needed to be free from all of that resentment inside of me.

One week after I turned twenty one I had a baby girl, Katelin Marie. I named her after my sister who died at birth. I've never felt so much happiness in my life, she was so perfect. It's a love you can't explain, so deep in your gut. My mom and my best friend never left my side while I was in labor, they were a great team for me.

Even though my stepmother was better to us during that time and I could really count on her for anything that pertained to Katelin, it still wasn't an ideal situation. She slept on a couch in the kitchen so if I needed to heat a bottle up for Katelin during the night, it would wake her up and she wasn't very pleasant about it. In the middle of the night I would heat her bottles up in the bathroom sink under warm water which took forever!

I finally made enough money to move out of my dad's and have a home to call our own. For several years I had to have a roommate to share expenses however, it made me feel more like a parent to live on my own.

It just encouraged me to keep striving for better and to be able to give my daughter the best life I was capable of.

Before Katelin came into my life I worked two jobs as a hairstylist and waitress. Being a waitress allowed me to promote my business as a stylist and make enough money to pay my bills. After Katelin

was born I had to give up the second job as a waitress so I could be home with her at night.
I had to rely on myself to make enough money to support her as a stylist. I received child support from her father but it was just enough to pay for daycare every week. I had to go without a lot but she was well worth it.

I felt as if my daughter saved me, perhaps that now I had a purposeful driven life!

We ate a lot of Ramen noodles and believe it or not as an adult, Katelin still likes Ramen noodles and so do I.

Whatever you desire in life will come if you believe it will and accept nothing less. I know the powerful word in the statement is BELIEVE.

Having a daughter
Brought life to a
Part of my heart
That I never
Knew existed.
 -Brenda Kosciusko-

KATELIN

Waiting for your arrival
After many months of fear
I was laying there wondering
If holding you was near.

Finally after a long day
That moment was here
I took one look at you
And your purpose became so clear.

My heart filled up with joy
My eyes with a tear
I couldn't have loved another
As much as I did you my dear.

Your hair was so blonde
Your eyes were so blue
Your skin was so soft
And I loved holding you.

Your tiny little toes
Your perfect feet
Your little nose
Perfection couldn't be beat!

-Tara Flaherty-

A Mothers trust

In 1995 I had a dream to own my own salon. I was only twenty-four years old and a single mother of my daughter who was three at the time.

Being in the business for five years and having to grow up so fast, I felt that I could handle the challenge.

I was so young and hadn't previously owned a home or a business so I couldn't get a loan. I asked my mom if I could borrow the money, she said, "Tara, if you can show me on paper how you can afford to own a salon then we'll talk."

So I wrote up a business plan with much enthusiasm, the right numbers and she believed in me!

That is when "Cuttin' it Close" became realistic to me.

It was such a challenge because the space was left unattended for quite some time. It was in a great location, however everything had to be renovated to make it into a salon and we had to do most of the work ourselves to meet our budget. We had a lot of hard work ahead of us, not only did Mom loan me the money but she was there every day to help me make my dream come true.

When my daughter Katelin was a year old my mom moved back to Ohio because she lost my stepfather when he was forty four from a massive heart attack. That was extremely devasting. We were so happy to have her with us again but sad for her loss as well. Another hard life altering heartache my mom had to endure. She's such a strong woman.

There's something I have decided that all of us human beings have in common 100% that we can't debate, argue or have a discrepancy about and that is we are all going to die and we have no idea when. So make your life a good one!

I enjoyed working with my mom everyday, she was always an inspiration to me and always taught me a lot. We had to use our manpower or should I say, "woman power!" I only borrowed $10,000 so we had to do most of the work ourselves. It was a challenging project, however we were very proud in the end.

The day I opened I only had $500 left in my bank account. Did that make me nervous?

Hell yes, but I knew I was going to make it work!

I met this man who was the maintenance man for the building and he said, "you are so young, aren't you scared to do this?" I said, "no, they can't take away the most important thing to me which is my daughter and the worst thing that can happen is I have to file bankruptcy!"

I wanted to build a good life for my daughter. I wanted her to be proud of me.

I'm thankful to Mom for believing in me and helping me make my dream come true.

Cuttin' it Close started on Ashland Road in Mansfield, Ohio. In the beginning it was just myself and one other stylist who was right out of beauty school so I had to teach her a lot. She was such a joy to be around. One time I let her cut hair on rollerskates, that was so hilarious! We worked hard but always found time for fun. I watched her grow to become a wonderful stylist, wife and mother.

The salon started with only three stations and 1200 ft.² of working space. As the salon grew with customers and stylists we just continued to add more stations.

After a while it was hard to do the work by myself. I thought how nice it would be to find someone to share the dream of mine with and help me maintain it as well.

I knew that would happen someday but until then I just kept building my empire.

The law of attraction is always there……

"Everything you want
is out there waiting
for you to ask.
Everything you want
Also wants you.
But you have to take
action to get it."

-Jack Canfield-

Another love

In November 1996 my girlfriend and I were out on the town having a great time when a man came up to me and said "I think we were supposed to be introduced to each other tonight." I knew there were a couple guys my friends wanted to introduce me to but we left the party before I was able to meet them. So I said, "are you Jim?" He said, "no", but his friend spoke up and said, "I am." I felt like a huge dork because as it turned out it was the wrong Jim. The other man spoke up and said, "my name is Leo", and I thought he was so cute! He was the other guy my friend wanted me to meet.

We talked and danced for a while and then we said goodbye.

The next day he called me at the salon and said, "if I let you cut my hair would you go out with me?" I thought that was pretty funny so I agreed to cut his hair. He wouldn't let me cut his hair short so that proved to me that he had a mind of his own. I liked that about him so I agreed to go out.

The next week we went on our first date to a dive bar right next to the salon. I didn't mind that because it was casual and safe.

There was just something about him, we could talk about life so easily. When we finished our date, he went to kiss me but he bit my lip instead! It didn't hurt but what was up with that? Talk about being mysterious!

The next weekend we went on another date to my sister's house to watch a movie. I thought we had a good time, however two weeks went by and I didn't hear from him.

I called the friend that knew both of us and she said she had heard that he thought I was too much of a prude for him. What? You can't be serious? I called him up and told him how much of a prude I was NOT! He laughed and told me why he thought that and then we made plans for another date.

He went through a divorce six months before he met me so having a serious relationship was not in the near future. He had a little two year old boy who was so cute and smart, however he was very shy but once he got to know me I think he started to like me a little. Leo was such a good dad and I admired that about him. He was sweet and patient with his son.

We had a good time dating but it wasn't getting too serious, he wasn't ready for all that. We were dating for about six months when history repeated itself and…

I found out once again that I was pregnant!

I couldn't believe it! I was so scared to tell him.

This time I thought I was in love and totally respected this man because he was always so honest with me. I knew where I stood with him.

Leo took it well but it was a long pregnancy by myself. I had a lot to focus on with having a five year old and running a business as a single woman. I did the best I could.

During my pregnancy my hearing kept declining more than ever and I didn't know why. I have always had ear problems since a little child but I never had this much trouble hearing. I went to the doctor and found out I had a serious ear disease called Cholesteatoma.

Cholesteatoma is a destructive and expanding growth consisting of keratinizing squamous epithelium in the middle ear and or mastoid process. Cholesteatomas are not cancerous as they may suggest, but can cause significant problems because of their erosive and expansive properties. This can result in the destruction of the bones of the middle ear as well as growth through the base of the skull into the brain. They often become infected and can result in chronically draining ears. Treatment almost always consists of surgical removal.

They couldn't do surgery until after I had my baby. It was very scary! I remember feeling lonely a lot while I was pregnant and couldn't understand why Leo didn't want to be with me. I had to work really hard on regaining my self worth.

I had a great support system, however I still had that sadness within me that I wasn't a good enough woman. I was about to have a second baby as a single woman without being married.

I decided to get my tubes tied after my baby was born because I never wanted to feel this way again. They made me go through counseling first but I was definite about my decision.

On May 3, 1998 Shelby Nicole was born. She was so beautiful with her vibrant red hair and blue eyes. She looked just like her dad but with red hair.

I was so happy and I felt that gut-aching love like I did with her sister, Katelin. She was perfect! I was the luckiest lady alive with two beautiful girls that were mine forever.

Leo was there with me and I felt that instant bond between us. He cried when she was born and fell instantly in love with her as well. I knew he was going to be a good father.

Three weeks after Shelby was born I had my ear surgery. They wanted to do it immediately after she was born but I wanted to breastfeed Shelby for at least a couple weeks. It was worse than they thought. I was in surgery for six hours. The disease had eroded through my bones of hearing so they had to put a prosthetic in and remove my mastoid bone. They saved my life again as this happened to me when I was seven on my other ear.

Six months later the disease came back so I had to go back for surgery again. I still couldn't hear very well so a year later they did another surgery and changed the prosthetic to titanium. I was grateful to Leo because he took care of Shelby and I during this time.

My ears are very delicate. I have to have tubes in them for the rest of my life and absolutely can not

EVER get them wet! Try being fifty years old and having a mother that still frets about you being in a canoe, raft, boat, swimming pool or possibly even a creek. Not fun! However in her defense I have been with drunk people around water that have no idea that they could possibly cause me harm by doing one stupid thing!

I'm aware of how serious my ear problems are but I try not to focus on the worst case scenario. I also try to express to others who have ear issues to not take it lightly. I could have possibly died if I would have disregarded my hearing issues.

After that year went by we all became closer. There had been so many nights of heartache, loneliness and feeling hopeless of wondering if we would ever be a family.

Leo finally asked me to marry him. Wow, what a shock that was! I nearly had a stroke because for almost a whole year he was dating other people so I finally did as well but nothing serious.

He put a stipulation on the engagement that he would like me to quit smoking and firm up my butt! That hurt me and hit on the self worth issues a little bit more, however I accepted the ring because I really wanted us to become a family.

We finally all moved in together. Another challenge we were about to conquer, as it is so hard to bring two families together. I knew what it was like being a stepchild so I never wanted his son to feel the way that I felt. I wanted to be the best version of a mom I could for him. I never wanted him to feel second best or unloved in any way.

I tried to teach Leo a lot about that because he did not come from a broken home. He was never a step-anything. I was a stepchild, step-granddaughter, stepsister and now going to become a stepmother. We had to overcome hard times between us over that and more.

I moved out for a short time because the adjustment was REAL, especially moving into his house. He had a hard time making me feel like it was mine as well. We finally bought a house together so that was much better for our relationship.

During the short time that I had previously moved out I decided to take on another challenge/adventure in my life....

"Blessed are the curious, for they shall have adventures."

Becoming extremely brave

In April 2001 I decided I needed to be the one chosen from the government, a group called ACDI VOCA, to go to Russia and teach them about our profession. It is a program that sends Americans to other countries to teach them different avenues in the vocational field.

I sent in my résumé and I was chosen! I was so excited! My mom was so nervous about me going that she tried to go with me. They declined that from happening.

I wasn't going to get paid to do the job but they paid for the whole trip. I was excited but a little nervous because I would be going by myself for two weeks. I've been traveling alone for years going back-and-forth between my parents but never to another country.

Boy did I hit the all-time bravery award this time!

I was a little anxious because it was going to be a long trip. Ten hours to Germany and then eight hours to Russia. I'm not the most patient person when I'm traveling because I can get hyper and my feet get fidgety.

When I arrived in Russia it wasn't your typical airport. We landed several feet away from the airport and there were men outside with weapons. You had to walk outside to get to a very small airport. People were crowded together and I couldn't see anyone that was supposed to be there waiting for me.

All of a sudden I heard my name being called in the distance, "Tara, Tara Burkepile." I raised my hand so the lady could find me. She took me to a private room and said It was a VIP room. Boy did I feel much better. That was my first experience of how the Russians made me feel so important.

I had a private driver that drove me four hours to the city of Tomsk. He couldn't speak English so that was a long drive.

I have to admit I've heard about the olden days but of course I've never seen them. Everything looked so old and out of date but the people, mainly women, look so young and beautiful. The cars were old and they drove very fast.

We stopped at a broken down village on the way there and the toilets were just a hole in a bench that went to the ground. That's when I got a little worried about how this was going to turn out. Good thing I grew up in the woods, I could pee in a hole no problem!

Well that was the beginning of a very interesting trip. After that, I had a round the clock interrupter unless I was in the bathroom or asleep. That was a little frustrating at times because he was pretty young and didn't really know the profession. I'm also very independent so I really wasn't a fan of someone constantly at my side, however we made the best of it. He was cool and a lot of fun.

The idea of staying in a luxury hotel was definitely out of the question. I was put in a dorm with college kids. I never went to a university but I can guarantee you that these dorms were nothing like the US. It was like staying in a box with one little window. The bed was so small that I could barely fit in it and I'm very small. No telephone!

The first shower I took was absolutely cold, cold, cold! The maintenance man came to fix it the next day and I literally had to hold my breath while I stood beside him because he smelled so bad. He was extremely nice and he gave me hot water so I handed him a $20 bill. He nearly fell over with gratitude because in Russia that was some peoples one-month pay. I was hoping that would help him out and he would possibly buy a bar of soap with it!

No really that's how bad he smelled. I was so grateful to make him so happy.

That seemed to be normal in Russia as they all have that body odor smell. I kept going to the bathroom to smell my armpits to make sure it wasn't me but it was clearly a normal smell for them. They wore their clothes multiple times to preserve the water there.

I couldn't believe how little people were paid. An average income was $30 a month. Haircuts ranged from $.50 to three dollars. They really had to work hard for their money.

I went to three different salons to teach and they all treated me like I was royal. I was on their national TV two times and was interviewed for their paper. I had the time of my life.

I lost ten pounds while I was there because the food wasn't that desirable. When we pulled into the city they had food huts instead of trucks and there was a hunk of meat hanging with flies on it. I asked if that was a normal thing and it was so I pretty much bypassed eating any meat the whole two weeks.

Of course I got home sick but what an experience to go through. Someday I would love to go back with my family and visit. I'm not sure if I taught them many new techniques because fashion is a big deal in Russia so they were already up to date.

I don't know how much they like Americans, however I can say that I inspired them with my happy, fearless, non-judgmental personality. They made me feel special so I guess it was a win-win adventure.

I'm so thankful that I listened to my instincts and took on that challenge as it was another step of independence and vulnerability for me.

"When you always try to foresee your future, It takes away the beauty of your journey".

-Tara Flaherty-

Taking a risk

In 2002, Seven years had gone by and my salon had grown at a nice rapid pace. More stylists were sent to me year after year so we had to continue to add more stations.

In the 90's we didn't have social media to help expand our business. Nor did we have cell phones and computers were so expensive to buy.

I built my business by getting involved with Miss Ohio, having community events, donating to every good cause, sponsoring little league teams and adult teams. Whatever the community needed we were there.

Word of mouth was the best advertisement along with paying the big bucks for an ad in the News Journal and telephone book. We did hair for the homeless shelter and became a sponsor every year at Christmas time.

I hired a receptionist and finally realized I needed a manager as well.

I hired Tammy, a lady that my friend referred to me as my manager. At first I felt as if she thought I was young and didn't know a lot. That didn't last long after I showed her a few wallpaper tricks that I learned from the best...my momma.

We bonded right away. I couldn't have asked for a better sidekick than Tammy as my manager. She was loyal, honest, an extremely hard worker and always had my back gracefully. I was the boss and she was boss-E. We all loved and respected her.

We had to expand upstairs, however that soon became a poor investment because the building was so old that the electric bill started to cost more than my rent. It didn't take me long to realize it was time to relocate into a place that was more economical and that I could call my own.

Many months went by searching for the right property while a lot of doors got slammed in my face. When you're dealing with the board of trustees you better have your shit together!

Especially if there are DUCKS QUACKING in the room getting to vote with no valid stance but only perhaps afraid of change!

I wasn't going to give up even though I had become mentally exhausted because when I get something in my mind, it doesn't go away until I make it happen.

That's when I learned what perseverance means. The ability to continue to strive for success in spite of difficulties or setbacks.

We were living in Ontario at the time and Leo and I were driving down Park Ave. That's when we noticed a big cool vacant building for sale that used to be a restaurant. You could tell it had been vacant for a while but I kind of got a warm feeling when we drove past it.

I was reluctant because it was several miles away from my current location and I wasn't sure how our clients would feel about the move.

I would be taking another risk that was uncertain and feeling very vulnerable.

We looked at it with no electricity and the smell of mildew took your breath away because it had been vacant for twelve years. With a leap of faith I made an offer.

This time I was a little scared as I could see there was so much work that needed done. Major rehab! We hired a few people to help and what a job! We worked so hard from April to August and finally got to the finish line.

Leo and I almost split up because we definitely ran out of money, energy, patience and kindness for each other. I'm surprised we stayed together to be quite honest. We both had a tremendous amount of stubbornness, strength and determination so I imagine that helped.

The day we opened we had both been up for twenty four hours straight so that we could open on time and pass all inspections. Of course we did pass and finally another dream came true.

The move was very successful because we were now centrally located, people from all over came to visit our salon. Clients would say it was very colorful, warm and inviting.

I was very proud and humbled of how it turned out.

IT WAS MY BEAUTIFUL SALON I ALWAYS DREAMED OF HAVING!

The future belongs to those
Who believe in the beauty
Of their dreams.
-Eleanor Roosevelt-

Dreadful fire

It was the following January 2003 when the phone rang at 1:30 in the morning. It was the security system telling Leo something about the salon. He jumped out of bed and said "I have to go, the salon is on fire!" We didn't know how bad it was so he left before me. I wrapped up our daughter in a blanket and put her in the truck to see what was happening for myself.

I was driving just two blocks away from the salon and I could see the smoke! My foot began to shake terribly so I could barely drive because I just knew it was bad!

As I pulled into the parking lot there were fire trucks everywhere. Leo was nowhere to be found. I was in shock! I sat there and watched smoke billowing out of my salon that we had just put our heart and soul into.

Finally, Leo came. He had gone back to the house to try to stop me from coming down because it was so bad. We both just couldn't believe it!

Leo kept going up to the building to see what was going on. The fire chief said they probably wouldn't know for a little while. Everything was ruined and the smell of that fire was unbelievable!

I could barely move now and could not find any words to say. My manager Tammy, who was also a very dear friend to me, heard about the fire on the scanner and came down. We just sat there and stared at the burning salon for a couple hours.

Leo kept walking back-and-forth to the salon and then to me. I know he was trying to be the strong one. I was just in shock!

Finally they told us to go home. There was nothing more to do. We needed to get some sleep because it was almost 4:30 in the morning. We came home and I laid there for a little while but couldn't sleep. I needed to call my family and my girls that worked at the salon before they got there or heard it on the radio.

That's when it hit me. I called my girl Charlie who was usually the first one in. I could barely talk because the emotions finally got me. I started to cry. It was very hard to call everyone and say the same thing over and over. I couldn't stop crying!

We went to the salon the next morning and as we pulled in the parking lot there were people everywhere. My employees, clients, another fire truck, friends and family. There were a lot of people crying so thankfully for some reason when people are upset I get strong. I was trying to keep my emotions together for everyone else until I went inside....

Oh my what a horrible smell! I would rather smell mildew! Water was everywhere and everything had a coat of black soot on it. If it wasn't burnt it was smoke covered. The product bottles looked as if they were minutes away from exploding!

The fire chief was there and made his decision that the fire started from a lamp in my office. The cord had a short in it. Leo was relieved when he knew it wasn't anything else electrical because he did all the rewiring in the salon. I, of course, never doubted his work!

We all went to breakfast to figure out what the next plan would be. I was still in shock but just living in the moment. We decided to have a meeting that night and lay out our options.

I became very ill, imagine that, with chest pains so the meeting had to resume without me.

That night I felt as if I couldn't do it again. Not mentally or physically. I just wanted to call it quits! The renovation the first time was so fresh in my mind that it literally scared the crap out of me!

The first time almost tore my family apart. We had just gotten back from vacation in Florida that was much needed for Leo and I because we literally were thinking about splitting up. Well I was anyway.

I decided to do what always works for me, sleep on it!

When I woke up the next morning I knew what my decision was....

Not yet! My dream is not over yet! Not like this. I want to say when it's over and it's not going to be from a fire. So I got up and got to work.

I called the insurance company to find out my options. Well it was a little devastating at first because my insurance agent forgot to change the contents policy from the old salon to the new salon. I was only covered for twenty thousand and we had seventy five thousand lost in contents. I was so distraught for a moment until she informed me that I had business interruption loss coverage. That meant that anything we needed to start up my business again would be covered. Thank goodness!! Leo was able to be my general contractor so I was relieved by that as well.

We found an old salon up the road that had been vacant for a couple years. It took two weeks and we were up and running in this temporary location. Things were good and we all worked together as a team.

I was so proud of my girls and the way they just carried on and did what we had to do to get by. We made a lot of fun memories but boy were we ready to get back into our salon.

It took about four months to renovate again and then we were back in business. You could still faintly smell the fire but it was more beautiful than it was the first time. I got to change the things that in the beginning I didn't have the money to do. That was probably the one and only good thing that came from the whole disaster.

I am a firm believer that there is always something good behind every bad thing you just have to find it!

Number one, nobody was hurt and number two I ended up having good insurance.

I know that life is better when you stay focused on what you want and you don't absorb your life with self-pity.

Perseverance!!

Soon after we reopened we became a very busy successful salon with twenty seven employees. We also became runner up for business of the year.

I couldn't have been more proud and very humbled once again!

Leo had become my rock during the devastating time of the fire and we became very close again. We got married nine months later on September 6th after being engaged for five years.

Our dream home

It was 2005 and Leo and I decided to make another dream come true. This time it was Leo's dream. We were going to build our own home.

We found a piece of property with ten acres of woods. We had to clear a lot of the trees out so we would go there almost every weekend and camp out. Those were really fun times, however a lot of work.

We put our other house on the market, well guess what? It was sold to the first people who looked at it. How amazing is that? It was a good thing we had our barn built already because that's exactly where we put all of our things.

We became homeless so we had to move in with Leo's parents. They took us in with our three children and our big Rottweiler for seven months. We were so thankful to them and I know after a while they were ready for us to leave because it was a zoo half the time! No more peace and quiet for them.

They were wonderful people and always had us in their best interest. However I was ready to be a mom again and for all of us to have our own space.

Leo worked hard and built us the most beautiful home I could ever ask for.

We had three major fights over building this house. One was the barn. I wanted a bigger one to have animals but he was worried about the cost and didn't want animals.

Second was the countertops, I wanted a rust red and he couldn't imagine it. Well we're both pretty stubborn and headstrong but he won the battles. I guess someone had to give in.

<u>The third battle was a little different. I was not going to lose….</u>

We had a beautiful front porch and I had a vision of how I wanted to do the landscaping with beautiful plants and flowers. He wanted grass. Can you imagine ladies? Grass? No way!

Well I had to fight for this one. I came outside to find him planting grass right up to the steps of our front porch. I was so upset I started yelling at him to please stop and he wouldn't.

I went inside to my bedroom and started to cry like a baby until something came over me and I said, "no way am I losing this battle!" I went back outside and……"temperamental tara" came out and I threw a shovel at him, thank God it missed him! I got on my hands and knees brushing away the grass seed. I was like a maniac!

I think he decided he wanted to live through the day so he finally let me win that battle.

Sometimes you win, sometimes you lose but if you fight for what you want then you usually will at least have a chance to win!

Building a house together was definitely a challenge and I'm surprised once again that we didn't get a divorce. We can be proud to say we did it and we had a very beautiful dream home on ten acres.

I was very grateful, however it was a lot to take care of. I know, I sound like a spoiled BRAT but it really was a lot more work! Bigger isn't always better, it just means more space and more work especially when you have a lot of people making messes.

I never minded hard work, however I may have gone a bit overboard on this next challenge knowing I couldn't even get my husband to do a load of laundry besides his hunting clothes. Just sayin….

"Somewhere along the way, we must learn that there is nothing greater than to do something for others."

-Martin Luther king Junior-

It's a chain salon

My motivation and vision scares me sometimes because I never know when it's going to stop. In 2007 Cuttin' it Close was going to become a chain. We found a vacant building in a subdivision in the next city over in Ashland, Ohio. It was right in the heart of Ashland University. Best location I could have found and very affordable. Let the renovation begin AGAIN!

Cuttin' it 2 Close became another reality. I realize this has always been a dream of mine, however I'm not quite sure it was just my dream that transpired the second location. My girls at the salon wanted this to happen just as much as me. The enthusiasm they had about it just kept giving me a bigger push to do it!

There were a lot of questionable hurdles I had to overcome to get this salon open. I worried that I would be gone from my family too much. I worried about not getting enough business. I was worried about not having enough help at home. I had to use almost my last penny to get the place started. This time I was a little scared but I didn't let my fears stop me. It was so much fun designing this salon.

After we opened it became another success. I got involved with the college and we set up a spirit table at all the home football games.

Getting involved with the community has always been my best source of advertisement. We pulled in a lot of college students from that just like I had hoped to do.

The only thing I really disliked about the location was that it was attached to a Subway Restaurant which in the beginning I thought would be an excellent idea. We could eat lunch there everyday and there would always be a potential client eating there, possibly in need of a haircut as well. Great idea right?

Well, only if you don't care about smelling like a big fat onion everyday! Not so cool. No amount of hair color or hairspray took that awful smell away unfortunately.

I worked at both locations and a couple of my girls from the big salon worked there as well. The excitement of something new has always been a thrill for me but maintaining has always been my biggest challenge.

Leo never held me back from my dreams, he always helped me get them started and was very supportive of my ideas. I have always appreciated him for that, however I feel he fell short on helping me maintain everything.

As you see I was manifesting everything I always dreamed of having in my life, however there was always something missing that was allowing me to feel unsatisfied.

It wasn't that I didn't feel gratitude but perhaps the complete opposite, possibly unworthy. Some sort of internal block...

Broken heart again

As I sit here and try to remember fifteen years ago I'm having a hard time deciding how to put this in the right words….

It was the year of 2008 I got a divorce. Yes, very sad based on all the challenges we went through. It was one of the hardest decisions I have ever made because I thought I loved my husband as much as I could have loved anyone.

I didn't talk about our personal challenges in the previous chapters, however we did have many. I begged him to go to counseling with me and he declined.

I went to counseling by myself which was very good for me because there was a lot more than just my marriage that I needed help with. I probably should have stayed in counseling my whole life because I feel that it's always helpful to have someone tell you what a shitshow you are!

Reflection is always what we need to maintain a healthy life. You know, someone to tell you "you need to do better." It's someone you can tell everything to and they TRULY are only trying to help.

Leo told me I was the only one that needed therapy. Maybe he was right, however when you're in a marriage it should be a team effort in learning how to understand each other better, perhaps from a professional's perspective. My counselor knew that I told my husband that if he didn't come with me at one point then we were getting a divorce.

So, it was my last session and I can remember sitting there waiting for him to show up. Hoping and praying that he would be vulnerable enough to listen to our dysfunction and want to fix it. My counselor waited to come down to get me a little bit longer than usual.

With tears in my eyes I knew what he was about to tell me.

My last session was him counseling me on giving me strength to follow through with my ultimatum. I couldn't keep threatening him and jeopardizing my own happiness, I had to value and respect my own self. I wanted to be treated with love and kindness, however the longer I stayed the more I felt like nothing I did was of value.

My self worth had become very compromised. I was very scared to be alone again. I felt naked!

About a month after we both agreed to get a divorce Leo finally decided he wanted to work on our marriage, that he would go to counseling. I felt as if I couldn't trust him anymore and he had already let me down so I had to stay strong to my decision.

It broke my heart to see him cry. It also felt good to hear him admit to his own convictions, however my mind was made up.

I don't want to talk bad about my ex-husband, he is a good man and I am a good woman, however we just grew apart and never dealt with our issues from the very beginning of our relationship.

I always felt like my self worth was compromised to begin with. Like I was never good enough.

Remember when Leo asked me to marry him and said he would like for me to quit smoking cigarettes and firm up my butt? Well, I could never accomplish either one of those requests and It always made me feel bad about myself.

I feel like maybe that's why I kept striving in my professional world but I paid a price for that in my personal world.

Building a big house wasn't exactly a good idea for us. That is another thing we didn't communicate to each other, neither one of us wanted a big house at that time we just thought the other did. Having two businesses with twenty-seven employees, a husband, three children, a Rottweiler and a big house to clean became extremely overwhelming for me to maintain with very little help. I felt like I was always letting someone down or feeling unappreciated.

I became mentally, physically exhausted and resentful. I hated to put my children through a divorce as I know what that feels like, however I didn't like them being in an unhealthy environment either.

We put each other through a lot of pain during our divorce. He wouldn't speak nice words to me for four years because he was in a lot of pain and angry at me. I wish it wouldn't have been that way as I am sure the main person it hurt the most was our daughter Shelby.

I would definitely not recommend animosity while going through a divorce. Put your kids first and your differences aside for the sake of your children's well-being.

Children are always watching us and if we want them to be good human beings then we should be living by example.

We had many good times, especially bringing our daughter into this world. Something else I will always be grateful to him for was that everytime I went to visit my dad I would come home crying because my stepmother would always make me feel like we were still less than. I didn't feel like we were important, but I wanted to have a good relationship with my dad. I loved him so much.

Leo told me that I either needed to find something I liked about her or that I just shouldn't go there anymore! I finally started to respect her love for animals. She took care of them better than anyone I have ever seen before.

I also have to admit that she loved my daughter Katelin dearly as well. She was definitely so much support when I lived with them while I was pregnant with her and she would always keep her at any given moment.

I decided from that day forward, I was going to just focus on that when I went for a visit. I felt our relationship became better so I made myself at home and didn't wait for her to make me feel any sort of way.

After that I maintained a pretty healthy relationship with her.

There were many things Leo and I did right, however as the years went by we lost sight of each other. I cannot say that I implicated everything in this next chapter to my marriage, matter of fact I realize now, there were many things I definitely could have done better.

The hardest challenge of my marriage was not feeling loved, valued or respected. When you do not tell your spouse you love them or nurture them, they will start to feel like a wilted plant dying of thirst. I imagine he felt the same way or he would've been happy and tried harder as well.

People are different and we all come from different upbringings, therefore it makes life a bigger challenge trying to understand each other. I came from a broken family and his family was still together.

My family showed a lot of affection and his family did not. How could the two of us understand each other without love and respect? We both had wonderful families but we experienced life in such different circumstances.

I would have stayed with my husband until death had I not become numb to the constant void of my mere existence.

Divorce is as hard as marriage because instead of you feeling dead, you grieve as if they had died. There were nights I missed what we once had so bad I could barely breathe crying myself to sleep, second guessing myself every step of the way. I knew that it was going to be hard but I prayed we would make it through and hopefully both become happier people someday.

In writing this chapter I feel that it has helped me grow and realize things I could've done better in my marriage. I feel it has made me understand the difference between a man and a woman's vulnerabilities.

I'm really not sure I could ever want to get married again, however I'm hopeful it will help me with my future relationships.

I don't really feel like many people are truly that happy being married, perhaps they just feel more safe, secure and need constant companionship or someone to nurture. Maybe that's what brings them joy, I don't know.

Or maybe it's not the marriage that makes them unhappy but perhaps it could possibly be they are not happy with themselves for various reasons.

I personally wish it looked and felt more desirable, perhaps worth the fight!

Leo asked me what I thought a marriage should be. It took me a while to answer but after deep thought it came to me in a simple, yet powerful poem.

When we decided to divorce I felt like a wilted plant dying of thirst. That was the best way I could describe to him how I was feeling...

Wilted plant- dying of thirst

To share

To tend

To care

To mend.

To listen

To hear

To glisten

To steer.

To see

To feel

To touch

To heal.

To share- A part or portion given to, or by, one person, one of equal parts.

Sharing is not just a material aspect of course you should share whatever it is that you have. It is the physical and mental part of sharing that is of importance; to share emotions, such as thoughts or feelings. To release anything that is on your mind that needs attention. To share responsibility is vital in a marriage. When one is slacking, the other should take over. Don't always have the same responsibilities because it is not fair to put more on one person. Take turns going to the grocery store and cooking. You get tired and want to be pampered too. When both people work, then it is important to share the rest of the responsibilities. It means a lot to notice what they are and that you are receptive to each other's needs. If one of you cooks, Don't just sit on the couch while the other cleans up the mess. If you want to be happy, help each other. Share.

"The game of life is the game of boomerangs. Our thoughts, deeds and words returned to us sooner or later, with astounding accuracy."

Florence Shinn (1871-1940)

To tend- To be directed; to look after.

Tend to your spouse's needs, wants and desires. Know what you both want out of life and help each other get there. Take care of each other mentally and physically. If one is having a bad day, try your hardest to make it better. Be nice and funny. Take time to play. Definitely always have sex and if you lose the desire, then talk about it and try to fix the problem. Kiss, touch and feel your spouse. You always need to feel loved. Sex is good but it is the foreplay that makes it better. It is all the little things that add up to make a big difference. So, get busy and tend to each other before it's too late.

"While we have the gift of life, it seems to me that only tragedy is to allow part of us to die whether it is our spirit, our creativity, or our glorious uniqueness."

Gilda Radner(1946-1989)

To care- A feeling of concern; to show interest or regard.

Find out what makes each other happy and show interest. There are no two people alike in this world, so you have to show some compassion and respect for the way the other person thinks and feels. You may not agree with it or want to do it, but it is important to take time to understand and nurture your spouse. Show that you care about that person's feelings. If she is crying, hug her and love her, the same for him. Talk to each other and respond to each other as best as you can. Be easy on each other when you're feeling blue. Remember what bothers one another and try not to do it. It is hard living together, so try to make it joyful and fun. Do nice things for each other. It doesn't matter if it is folding her clothes or cooking him a meal, just do it.

"Three things in human life that are important: the first is to be kind. The second is to be kind. And the third is to be kind."

Henry James (1843-1916)

To mend- To fix, repair- to correct.

When there are problems, fix them. Don't let them go until you can't see the light anymore. If something doesn't feel right then it must need attention. When you fight, make it right. Don't say I don't want to talk about it anymore, because it is important that you get it all out or I can assure you that it will come back out and it will feel even worse the second, third and fourth time you fight about it. If you don't solve your problems you will get a divorce eventually. When your spouse threatens to leave all the time it means they are not happy. Find out why and fix it. Solve your problems immediately!

"Keeping score of old scores and scars, getting even and one upping, always make you less than you are."

Malcolm Forbes (1919-1990)

To listen- To pay attention to what one is saying.

We all try so hard to get someone to listen and hear what we are saying that we lose sight of what is really happening. We twist things around to our own benefit because we don't listen to what is really being said. You can stop this by truly listening to what your spouse is saying. Don't think about what you're going to say next. When someone is talking, just take the time, focus and listen. When you have to talk in desperation to get the other person to listen, it is very emotional and upsetting. If you don't stay calm, you will miss something of great importance that the person you love is trying to tell you. Be patient and remember that you're not always going to agree and that is OK, just listen.

"One never knows what each day is going to bring. The important thing is to be open and ready for it."

Henry Moore (1898-1986)

To hear- To perceive by the ear; to listen with careful attention.

You're hearing is a gift from God. We take these things for granted most every day. When you can't hear it is frustrating, believe me, I can testify to that. But what is even more frustrating is when you don't hear each other. You can tell so much about a person by listening to the tone of their voice, whether they are sad, mad, happy, sick or tired. When you love each other, you hear these things. If you lost your site tomorrow, all that you would be able to rely on is your hearing. Be attentive to each other and hear the voice that is communicating with you.

"Be life long or short, its completeness depends on what it was lived for."

David Starr Jordan (1851-1931)

To glisten- To shine softly as reflected by light.

Be happy and you will glisten. When you are in love, you glisten. Anyone who is truly happy will glisten. You will see the sparkle of light in their eyes. Make sure you take the time to make sure each other is glistening. Love is a beautiful thing and the way you see it is through someone's eyes. Smiling is glistening, laughing is glistening it is free but worth a million bucks. If you love each other, then say so. Always say nice things and I guarantee you you will see a smile with a light in their eyes.

"When you reach for the stars you may not quite get one, but you won't come up with a handful of mud either."

Leo Burnett (1891-1971)

To steer- To guide in the right direction.

When one gets off track, the other is there to grab the wheel. Life is one big ride and we always lose sight of which path to drive down but if you work together, you will always find your way. It is hard when you are lost by yourself. Sometimes you just want to be the passenger. When you are behind the wheel, you're in control but eventually you will get tired and fall asleep, so you need someone else to take over. It is OK, there's always only one driver and one passenger. Change it up and make it a safe and enjoyable ride.

"You take people as far as they will go, not as far as you would like them to go."

Jeanette Rankin (1880-1973)

To see- To have the power of sight; to understand; to experience; to imagine; to predict.

Pay attention to what you see or you will miss something very valuable. What you don't hear, you will see. If your spouse looks great, tell them. If they look sad, hug them. Your sight is also a gift that we take for granted. Sometimes we get a blurry vision but it will always come back if we are happy. Take time to see each other for who you really are. No two people see things exactly alike. Everyone's vision is different. If one says the sky is gray, it is because that is the way their eyes see it. It doesn't mean you are right or wrong, it means they see it differently. It is very simple.

"A moment's insight is sometimes worth a life experience."

Oliver Wendell Holmes (1809-1894)

To feel- To explore, examine or perceive through the sense of touch; to perceive as a physical sensation; to believe; to consider; to be aware of; to be emotionally affected by.

To feel is so interesting because it can mean so many different things in so many different ways. To feel compassion, sorry, happy, love, hate, hot, cold, hard and soft. There are things you feel emotionally and physically. Listen to each other's emotions. Feel each other physically. When you learn to feel you will heal. When you go through life not feeling anything for other people, you will become so empty and numb. You have to be in touch with your feelings or you will be old and bitter before you know it. One thing that is hard to live with in a marriage is not knowing whether your spouse feels the love that you do. You must always share the way you feel because not knowing is harder than the truth.

"I have found that if you love life, life will love you back."

Arthur Rubinstein (1887-1892)

To touch- To allow a part of the body, as the hands, to feel or come into contact with; to join; to come next to; to have an effect on.

When you are touched in a soft, loving way it is calming. You can stop any bad emotion with one hand. Hold it out to the one you love. When you are loved you should touch them in a way that stops time. When you make love, touch each other like you mean it. Kiss each other- this means more than sex. Touching and kissing create more feelings of love than anything. Don't make your spouse long for affection. When we were babies it was a touch of our parents that calmed us. Just because we grow up doesn't mean that we stop needing the touch of love and comfort.

"There's nothing like a newborn baby to renew your spirit- and to buttress your resolve to make the world a better place."

Virginia Kelly (1923-1994)

To heal- To restore to good health; to mend.

To love is to heal. The power of love is unbelievable. When you are fighting for your life, it is love that you need. Heal the heart and make amends on everything. Don't let problems that you have become unsolved. Talk about things and try to make them better. Dry up tears, don't create them. Sadness is a dark place to be in. The only way to be happy is to heal yourself. When you are married you have to heal together or one will always be sad. Go to counseling if you need to, sometimes someone else can see things that you couldn't. If you don't heal your wounds, they will always break back open and become infected.

"I would not waste my life in friction when it could be turned into momentum."

Frances Willard (1839-1898)

It is not too late if you want, or think you can save your marriage. In my case, it was too late, but for yours it may not be.

I'm well aware that there's a lot more to marriage than just what I wrote but it's just my perception on how it could possibly be enhanced.

Thank you for allowing me to share my perspective on what I think a marriage should be with you, as it has helped me with my healing process.

I feel as if we are supposed to enhance the growth in one another. Make each other better people not just for our own benefit but enhance the happiness of one self. Allow each other to be the beautiful self that god created us to be as an individual.

"Life is a great big canvas;throw all the paint on it you can."
Danny Kaye (1913-1987)

A lot can happen in a marriage. To this day I do not regret my marriage nor do I regret my divorce. I only wish we would have tried harder to acknowledge, nurture and empathize with each other as individual human beings.

I loved being married. I just didn't love the emotional mess of it!

**"A HAPPY MARRIAGE IS
A LONG CONVERSATION
WHICH ALWAYS SEEMS
TOO SHORT."**

-Andre' Maurois-

I wrote this next poem about two years prior to my divorce that I would like to share with you. It was also chosen and printed for our local news journal on Mother's Day seventeen years ago.

It was right after we built our beautiful home.

I was sitting on our porch enjoying nature, and the beautiful landscaping I was able to create when the words came to me so easily…..

So Many Days

As I sit here on my porch with the wind blowing my hair, listening to the birds chirp, I begin to appreciate the life I have to share.

So many days I take for granted being a mom and a wife. When really it's a great reward and I wouldn't want another life.

So many days of feeling frustrated to be who they want me to be, when really it's my own fears of failure that hide the real me.

So many days of feeling depressed because there may not be enough, when really if I looked within, it's my family that makes me tough.

So many days of feeling anger for something that they've done, when really if they're happy then the battle is already won.

So many days of joy, it means so much to me, when really without them, where would my life be?

-Tara Flaherty-

Feeling freedom

After my divorce it became clear to me that I was searching for some peace in my life. I decided to sell my second location, Cuttin' it 2 Close. I only had it for two years, however having two locations became very hard to manage as a single mother. I needed to spend more time with my children as they were growing up entirely too fast.

It didn't take long to sell it because it was in a great location and everything was only two years old with a decent clientele. I doubled my investment so that made me happy. I felt a sense of relief after that, however there was still a sense of peace I was searching for.

I then decided to sell the big salon as well. A lady who worked for me wanted to buy it. I was apprehensive because she had no experience, however who was I to judge as I had no experience in the beginning of my journey as well. I took the offer and I was thrilled with the freedom I had gained. I felt like I could finally breathe.

It's very hard being in business for a lot of women. They can be very dramatic and hard to please. Everything has to be perfect. I lost myself along the way with always having to be enough for someone else other than myself.

Employees don't know the pressure we go through as business owners. They only see the money coming in but have no recollection of the money going out. Some of them always look for what needs done rather than what has been done. Or they just simply do not understand that we have a personal life as well as they do. It was a lot of stress making all of these employees happy. Clients as well.

One day I came into the salon to a ripped shampoo chair. Nobody would say how it happened. I didn't have it replaced for a while because I couldn't afford it at that moment so I used some black tape and you could barely tell it was there.

One of my employees kept making comments that it needed fixed and that clients were complaining about it. Come to find out, that same employee was the one who ripped it with her stilettos by putting her feet up on the chair while having her eyebrows waxed.

No accountability!

I sold the business but kept the building and she rented it from me. We had a land contract agreement on the business so I didn't get any money upfront. Big mistake! I wanted my freedom so bad that I trusted everything would work out.

When I sold the salon it had twenty three employees and was a thriving business. I was smart and put in my contract that if she put the business in jeopardy in any way that I could get the business back. Let's just say when I got it back there were only thirteen employees left and it was in financial ruin within two years. What a mess!

My lawyer advised me to change the name so I wouldn't be liable for any of the debt she had accumulated from the IRS. I went from point A to Z to save the salon.

I borrowed money from my mom again, only this time I wasn't so sure I could pay it back. I had also lost my spark. I didn't want it back, however I didn't want to lose everything I worked so hard for. When you really want something your desire is so clear and focused.

When I first started this salon I had such passion and motivation that I was unstoppable. It felt different this time. I was trying to save a sinking ship that nearly killed my spirit.

My inspiration was gone and I couldn't get it back no matter how hard I tried!

I always had a great support system with most of my employees, family and friends so that was never a problem. It was me, I had lost my passion. I tried as much as a person could do to save a sinking business with absolutely no money.

<u>*When you lose your desire and passion for something then you stop manifesting and the universe gets confused on what you are asking for.*</u>

The economy was horrible at this time, I tried to refinance only to find out my building was only appraising for half of its value. I owed more on it than it was worth. The parking lot needed to be paved, the basement was flooding like Noah's Ark and the retaining wall was about to cave in.

During this time my father was diagnosed with cancer and died thirteen months later. I really became depressed and sick. I felt hopeless. I realized that losing my father at sixty two made me certain that life could be very short.

After trying to bring the salon back for almost three years I made a decision to file bankruptcy. Who would have known that the comment I made back in 1995 to the maintenance man who is a dear friend to me now would have actually come true. I didn't want to be a failure however my health had become compromised due to all the stress.

We closed the salon, everyone was very sad, however I know it was the right decision for me personally. I didn't know where life would take me next, however I knew I was getting closer to the feeling of peace I longed for in my life. I didn't want anyone feeling sorry for me because I knew something was going to be better for me in my future.

I went back to the original salon I started and worked with a couple girls that used to work for me upstairs until I could figure out what I wanted to do next. I felt safe there as I could finally just focus on myself. It was strange not having so many responsibilities, perhaps a breath of fresh air.

I was there for two-and-half years and had enough of a break and realized I missed having my own place. A lot of my clients didn't like it there mainly because it was on a second level. They were also used to the way I ran my business in my own place. It was a part of me for so many years.

So I went on another adventure to find the perfect space for a few girls and I. I looked at a space that right away I knew was not it. The man that showed it to me offered to show me another space that he thought would be a great fit for us. I felt the connection right away when I walked in and I met the man that owned the building. Apparently he knew me and all about my story as he was a client that came to one of my girls at the big salon that I had to close.

He offered me the deal of a lifetime....

I really didn't have the money to invest in opening another salon but I had the desire!

He offered to do all the work and pay for it to turn it into a salon for me. I didn't even have to paint a wall!

I was so blessed and humbled by this. Normally I would have to work so hard and almost go broke before all of my past businesses were completed. Did I truly manifest this blessing? What a wonderful feeling that someone believed in me so much that I would be a great fit for his investment.

I named it TaraTherapy Salon & Art Studio. I felt that was fitting because as stylists, we should also earn a therapy certificate as well. This time I kept it small and had no employees. Everyone is a booth renter and they work for themselves. All of my girls at the salon pay me to work there, what a wonderful situation.

My daughter Katelin will be thirty one this year. She's now a stylist and I get the pleasure to work with her any day I wish to. She's become one of the best women I know.

We've been there for eight years now. I love it and hope to retire one day and perhaps my daughter Katelin could take over. Only if that is her desire as well. I'm so grateful that I have my own salon again with very little stress.

I wouldn't trade the journey I went through for any amount of money, however I'm proud of what I built for myself. Had I known what the outcome was going to be back in the beginning of this adventure, I can say I would still do it over again. Well, not all of it but I would still want to take that risk of fulfilling my dreams.

I paid my mom back every penny that I owed her. That was important to me. Sometimes I would help weed her flower beds and get yelled at for "wasting dirt", however I was willing to do anything to repay her. I also paid her phone bill for several years so I always made sure I paid my debt even to my mother.

Repaying people should always be a priority in our lives!

Over the past twenty eight years I've had many people work for me. I like to think that I inspired most of them in some way. I always tried to encourage each and every one of them to just be the best that they were capable of being.

I still have my rock steady "Nelle" after all these years. My last original employee. She has made me feel settled and I have always encouraged her to not be afraid of change. "Thank you my friend for always standing beside me!"

Perseverance molds you into becoming a better person.

There are no failures, only lessons learned are the biggest successes!

It helps you make progress even when things get tough and messy which is important for your future to become successful.

There will always be an obstacle or a setback however in order to be good at leadership you will need to know what perseverance feels like, continuing to get back up in spite of difficulties or setbacks.

Finding solutions for your challenges with grace and gratitude.

"Every adversity, every failure, every heartbreak, carries with it the seed of an equal or greater benefit."
-Napoleon Hill-

That was my time of waking up naked many times feeling very vulnerable in the business world.

The next segment of my life with new relationships is a true test of finding out who you are. What you want and definitely what you don't want…..

It's a whole new world!

"Being our messy,
Imperfect, authentic selves
Helps create a space
Where others feel safe
To be themselves too.
Your vulnerability can be
A gift to others.
How badass is that?" -B. Oakman-

Don't be afraid to....

MOVE AWAY

HAVE CHILDREN

OPEN A BUSINESS

BUILD A HOUSE

START OVER

WRITE A BOOK

TAKE A VACATION BY YOURSELF

STAND ALONE

OR FALL IN LOVE......JUST LIVE YOUR BEST LIFE!

My Journey through singlehood

New relationships

It has been fifteen years now since I went through my divorce. I have been in several relationships that didn't last, however each one has taught me something new about myself, perhaps what I'm looking for or what I'm not looking for.

The hardest part of being single during middle age is finding someone who is not emotionally damaged from a previous marriage or relationship. As a middle aged adult the desire for sex is also a necessity. I feel that some married people take this aspect for granted.

Single people are very vulnerable and feel uncomfortable with just having a sex partner. As a woman I have had to learn that meeting my needs is not a terrible thing as long as I don't put myself in a dangerous situation emotionally or physically.

Why is it that when a man has sex with a random person it's the walk of "fame" but for a woman it's the walk of "shame?" I'll never understand that nor will I accept that for my own life views.

The first man I dated was during and after my divorce, and Yes, with conviction I have to admit to this. He wasn't the reason for our divorce but I started seeing him while in the middle of it. I do NOT recommend this to anyone, however he is who brought me back to life from feeling like a wilted plant.

There wasn't anything he wouldn't do for me and told me how he felt about me all the time. We had so much passion for each other and he kissed me all the time. He had been divorced for a year and was still very resentful about it. Apparently he didn't treat his ex-wife very nice so I know he had regrets.

He tried so hard to be different to me but the demons of his past, not just with his wife but childhood as well, were still clearly in his head so he drank a lot to ease the pain. I tried to help but needed to deal with my own emotions at the time. I learned that I didn't want to fight to be right anymore. I was a fighter in my marriage and was exhausted from that.

The second relationship was very short, he had never been married and had no children. He had just split up from a four year relationship and was still exhausted from the mental challenges from her I suppose. He lived in the country so we went for walks in the woods, hunted mushrooms, had fires and would ride quads in the mud, all the things I truly enjoy.

We had a lot of fun and built a great friendship but couldn't connect in the love aspect. He made me become more comfortable with myself and let loose to try new things, however there was one new thing he wanted me to try out that I was not comfortable with at all. He said he called one of his ex girlfriends to see if she would be interested in doing a three way with us!!! What the hell? I had already told him "NO" on that one, I'm not ok with sharing my man!

The third relationship was my first high school love of four years from almost thirty years ago. He had just gotten divorced and was extremely bitter about it. At the time we hadn't spoken in eighteen years so it was nice to rekindle that relationship. He lived on a farm so I totally enjoyed going to visit him.

One night his cows got out and I got to help herd them back into the fence. That was cool bringing back my farm life memories. We had a nice time getting to know each other as adults but he was in no shape to trust and love someone again anytime soon. I realized at that time you can just be friends with an old love and wish them well and mean it.

The fourth relationship was a man who just got hurt from a very long relationship that ended so abruptly. We did a lot of hanging out with friends and spent a lot of time talking about life but never could connect with any emotions for one another.

He made me realize how strong and independent I was. He appreciated that about me but I think he liked the idea of taking care of a woman. That would have been a much better match for him.

He also expressed that passing gas in front of him would definitely be a reason to break up. Well, based on the fact that as the women get older in my family they seem to get the walking farts so I felt that would be a good reason to exit out before that happens to me!

The fifth relationship was a man that I completely fell for the moment I laid eyes on him. He was going through a divorce and had been separated for nearly a year. He was married to a woman that apparently needed him to function in life so I felt like my independence would be a breath of fresh air for him. Boy was I wrong.

He made me realize to never let a man know you don't need them even if you don't. That relationship put me through some pain but I was hopeful, based on his current indecisive life, he would have some regret and miss the peaceful relationship we had. There will be a chapter completely on him later.

The sixth relationship I had was with a man that I had dated briefly in my early twenties. At the time I was feeling very vulnerable because the relationship with the previous man that I fell madly in love with had broken my heart.

He made me feel safe and loved. We actually got engaged very quickly but it didn't take me long to realize he wasn't the man for me either.

Yes, I had other short term relationships in between in the past 15 years, however I will never stop putting myself out there and give up on finding a compatible love relationship for my life.

I'm happy being me and never want to just settle for anyone or be that person who hates love perhaps because they don't love themselves.

I also tried online dating a couple times and that was pretty funny. First time was through "match" and out of about a hundred guys contacting me I narrowed it down to three guys.

First one was a farmer and although I loved my father and respected his hard work on a daily basis, I was well aware of that type of lifestyle. I love to travel so that was a, "no go!"

Second guy had way too many young kids. I love kids but I also know what that type of lifestyle would entail as well, especially when my girls are grown, so that was another, "no go!"

Third guy I ended up giving my number to and within fifteen minutes he was sending me a picture of his "package!" Definitely a BIG time, "no go!"

I understand people meet and fall in love everyday from those sites as I appreciate that, however for me it just feels like a horrible interview process and gives me way too much anxiety. Matter of fact my sis, Heidi, met her fiancé on a dating site and we love him.

She is happier than I've ever seen her. Living her best life!

So you see... just because you get a divorce doesn't mean you're going to meet someone who doesn't have issues or find your knight and shining armor. I always communicate that to my friends and family that come to me for support while they are going through hard marital problems.

On the contrary I get accused of being the influence for divorce because I'm single and that is just not the case or fair to say the least. I have grown a lot since my divorce.

Most of you may be wondering if I regret ever getting a divorce. I have to answer that honestly with conviction. I wish I would have known who I was back then and expressed my emotions with a little more grace at times, however had we not, then maybe we both wouldn't have become the better people that we are today.

I do know this, I will not settle for a man that is less than my ex-husband. And I am proud to say that I never gave up on developing a healthy relationship with him to raise our daughter as peacefully as we could for her well-being. We went through very dark times though so it was not easy, but we both always wanted what was best for our daughter.

I have no idea how the second half of my life will go, however I refuse to hide behind any bitterness and just take one day at a time to continue to grow and be at peace with who I am and the decisions I make for myself.

Timing is everything, if it's meant to happen it will, at the right time for all the right reasons.

On the contrary, sometimes timing is painful and hard to understand why someone has to go through so many hardships in their life to find the strength that they never thought they had....

*"LITTLE BY LITTLE,
WE LET GO OF LOSS....
BUT NEVER LOVE."*

*"When someone you love
Becomes a memory, the
Memory becomes a treasure."
-unknown-*

Charlie

I have a very special girlfriend that I've been friends with since 1990. Charlie and I worked together as stylists for a long time throughout the years. She was working for me during the fire at my salon and had watched me go through a lot of challenges in my life through the years.

One day she told me that she didn't know how I was able to be so strong all the time. My reply was, "you are strong as well, you just haven't been through anything yet to show you how truly strong you are".

Well I will tell you shortly after that conversation, I can't even imagine how she didn't lose her mind with all the heartache she had to endure without God there to help her!

Charlie found out she was pregnant with twin boys and at sixteen weeks she had to go on complete bed rest. I know that was a challenge for her because she was a very busy successful stylist, wife and mother to a four year old son.

She went into labor at twenty seven weeks and sadly lost James within two hours and Eugene was born with multiple health issues. He had to be in the hospital for five months fighting everyday for his life.

The doctors told her that Eugene would be on a feeding tube the rest of his life and would most likely never walk or talk. Charlie did not take that for an answer, she put him in every kind of therapy she could, starting at a very young age to give him the best life they could.

I witnessed a strong vibrant woman take control of her life and refuse to just listen to what the worst case scenario would be. I watched my beautiful friend become a strong resilient eagle. So full of hope, grace and determination. She gave anyone who knew her inspiration.

Ten years ago when Eugene was only eight years old, she got that horrific phone call that her husband, just a month after his fortieth birthday, had been in an accident and that he didn't survive! It was so traumatic that I can't even find the right words to describe as I'm writing this.

Her husband "T" was a wonderful man loved by many. All I could do was go be with her to give her as much comfort as I could. When I walked into her house it was so full of sadness yet so full of love at the same time. There were so many people there giving her support. I couldn't leave that night. I just knew I needed to stay with her. She needed that comfort and I was able to do that.

We slept in their bed together and I couldn't wrap my brain around what just happened so I know she was in complete distress! All I could do is just pray for her and her boys.

The next morning she was tending to Eugene's daily routine as she always would. So strong and determined to be the best mother regardless of her despair. Completely amazing!

Her husband "T" was the love of her life. They had a marriage that I admired so much. You know, one that made it look desirable! Not perfect as they had their hard moments but they were in love and created a great life together to raise their boys.

They were always a joy to be around and just enjoyed life regardless of their challenges with Eugene. They never wanted anyone to feel sorry for them in any way. A very resilient couple.

Over the years Eugene has been diagnosed with Cerebral Palsy, Hydrocephalus, Autism, feeding tube since birth and many other health altering issues. Charlie continues to get him the best care along with constant love and support.

Eugene walks, talks and his smile lights up the room. He is smart and has the funniest personality. He loves to cus and make people laugh. His disabilities are hard on Charlie at times because he can be a handful. He will always be in her care or the care of someone else.

Charlie has a lot of support, however there are moments that I'm certain she feels helpless and all alone yet she still gets up everyday and puts on her happy face to face the world. Especially with our profession. Not only do we make people look better but we have to make them feel better too. It can be brutal when you feel miserable yourself!

Charlie is still young and full of life. She never stops putting herself out there to possibly find love again. Now she has to find enough love, not just for her but Eugene as well. Not to mention I'm sure Frank, her oldest boy, is probably right there analyzing the situation if someone is going to be good enough for his momma and brother. They are a rock solid family and have persevered through such a tragic experience.

I know there are times that Charlie doesn't even want to get out of bed but she does! She has surpassed the strength test way beyond mine.

Our friendship has gone through some challenges as well, however there is nothing that will make us lose sight of the love, respect and admiration we have for one another.

She is an inspiration to many women. Well those that aren't jealous of her because she's a beautiful single woman. Just sayin! There is nothing she can't overcome and knows her husband is watching over them and is very proud as he is with them in spirit.

She has woken up naked feeling very vulnerable to what her future holds many times, however she never stops believing there is a higher power that gives her the strength she needs on a daily basis.

Charlie soars like an eagle!

There is a part of me that feels as if "T" always knew deep down in his soul that he was going to die young, perhaps instincts he couldn't understand…..

He battled his life with Charlie from the beginning, however after their first date he told his mom he was going to marry her.

Then out of the blue he called off their wedding at first for no explained reason, he battled her on having more children for no explained reason and the one battle he won was getting an indoor dog months before he died.

Charlie was a little OCD at times and didn't like the idea of dog hair in the house. She was also a scaredy-cat at night. I can remember the night "T" died when she mentioned how safe she felt having their dog (Tanner) in the house and that she was so grateful to have him there now.

Oh, how our journey in this life can be one complete mystery!

"Only people who are capable of loving strongly can also suffer great sorrow, but this same necessity of loving serves to counteract their grief and heals them."

-Leo Tolstoy-

Who am I

"When you become single for whatever reason, you feel naked and very vulnerable."

The first step is figuring out who you are and what you want for your life. To become the best version of yourself.

VULNERABILITY
- Courage
- Good state of mind
- Ability to become resilient
- Not weakness or insecurity
- Potential growth in yourself and others
- Taking chances in spite of rejection
- Accountability
- Being authentic with others
- Trust
- Feeling difficult emotions: shame, guilt, grief or fear
- Reconnecting with people that have hurt you.

Being vulnerable builds greater strength, stronger relationships, and improves your self acceptance. It allows you to become more authentic and confident with who you are and accept yourself in every aspect. The more accountable we are for our own flaws the easier it is to grow from them and accept others for their flaws as well.

This is who I am....

MOTHER
Let's start with the good stuff. The blessed aspect of me is being a mother of two beautiful women and I would not trade that journey for anything. They are my life's most cherished treasures. They are who I strive to do better for my whole adult life.

I was scared to death to become a mother and I'm fearless. I didn't know if I was going to do everything right but I always knew that I would love them with all I had to give. Like I said when I had them, "it's a love so deep in your gut!"

While I was raising them I worried about every little detail from keeping them safe all day to making sure they woke up every single morning. I loved to watch them sleep as It brought me the most peace I've ever felt before.

Now that they are adults I just pray that they are safe, loved, happy and always know that I'm just a phone call away and wish for nothing more than for them to have a great "green" day!

KIND

I want to share my thoughts of me as an individual. I feel as if I'm very kind and would share anything I have with anyone who needs it. Matter of fact my girlfriend calls my home the "hotelTaraflaherty ", it's a woman's sanctuary. I try to help other women find their self worth, however I can be a hot mess myself at times so I'm not sure why they actually think I'm such a safe haven haha.

My girlfriend came to stay with me while she was separated from her husband, she really didn't have a lot of family members that she could go stay with like her husband did. I was her family.

They both meant a lot to me as we had been friends for a very long time so I tried to just listen and not take sides. In the end I got treated as if I did by a lot of people that I adored. That is very hurtful so I'm glad I kept it together and still treated everyone with kindness when I would see them regardless if I sensed any animosity. I know who I am and know that people just want someone to blame when they are hurting.

I actually felt in my heart that it would come to this one day. They were so different, my girlfriend was always trying to find herself and her husband was always afraid to try new things. One was always being vulnerable and the other was afraid to be. One was always trying to find the light and the other one was always afraid the light was going to burn out.

They married very quickly and had to learn all of these things while trying to raise children without really knowing themselves. They went through many challenges throughout their marriage of twenty years. I was there with them for a good portion of it and I will always admire both of them.

When people get a divorce it breaks my heart to see how it affects so many that have been close for years. You don't have to choose or blame. It's hard on everyone but it is their business not anyone else's to judge.

Acts of kindness can come in many ways. Lending a hand, helping someone who's struggling physically or emotionally or just simply being in someone's presence when they need you the most. Those are the kind things I enjoy doing the most. It doesn't have to be of monetary value.

I believe the more generous and grateful you are, the more bountiful your life will be!

LOVING

When I love someone, I love them very much. There isn't anything I wouldn't do for someone I love or really anyone in my life for that matter. That also has been a very difficult lesson for me as well.

When you have a lot of people in your life it can become quite overwhelming with trying to be there for everything and everyone. Once a day I check on someone I love or someone I know that is having a difficult time and tell them I love them.

Sometimes you never know how you're going to impact someone who could be struggling from something and how much your words mean to them.

I wish people truly knew my heart and how much I want people to know how special they are. There are only so many hours in a day to do what I have to and decide who needs tended to the most.

 I don't ever want to stop loving people. However, if I distance myself from people it is for these certain reasons. I just need a break from uncomfortable energy, I feel disrespected and unappreciated or I just lost respect for you as the kind of person I thought that you were. Or perhaps life gets in the way but when we see eachother again life resumes as if time hadn't passed at all.

If I love someone it takes a lot for me to let go so perhaps I just had to realize I need to set more boundaries that's all.

I've had my heart broken a lot in the past at times not just from men in my life but family and friendships as well. I feel as if they expect a lot more out of you if you're single and have a difficult time understanding that the expectations of me and themselves should be of equal value.

I've always put more expectations on myself than others therefore at times I end up feeling very hurt. I know I've hurt people as well, that's when I realized I just had to communicate the boundaries I set for myself in a better manner. I'm trying to be more accountable, do better and grow from it.

Friendships can be work just like a marriage. Sometimes they can be painful but they are supposed to make you grow as well. I don't know what I would do without my friends in my life at times while being single now for fifteen years. I am a good friend and I do my best to express that part of me and still remain vulnerable even if it's been a painful experience at times.

I want to share another poem that I wrote at a very young age about what friendship means to me….

A friendship to me

When someone cares
About your deep dark fears
and is hurting inside
When you are in tears.
When someone understands
When you do something wrong
And you feel it's the end
But they're with you all along.
When someone smiles
And makes your heart lighter
And make the dullest days
Always seem brighter.
When someone is there
With nice things to say
And you know you can depend on
With each passing day.
When someone stands by you
Until the very end
You know that someone
Is a very special friend.
-Tara Flaherty-

It was published in a poetry book almost twenty years ago.

FORGIVING

I'm very forgiving and that is for my own soul and what is expected from God. Forgiveness doesn't mean you have to have those people in your life if you feel they would continue to hurt you, however you can still keep them close in your heart.

The best example of me being forgiving would be when my sisters and I found out from our mom that six years after my dad died my stepmother had put the family farm in my stepsister and husband's name. They were put on the deed and never even discussed it with us!

To be honest we always knew something like this would happen because our stepmother would never let us have anything. Not even our childhood things that belonged to us. She was an extreme hoarder that couldnt get rid of anything.

When it finally happened, it was so painful. My oldest sister Lori asked my stepmother why this was happening and her reply was, "your father didn't want you girls to have anything!" My sis said, "How dare you, my father would never ever say something like that, I never want to see or speak to you again!"

It's a fifty acre, four generation farm that was to stay in the family per my dads wishes.

Now, my stepsister has been in our lives since she was five years old so we would have never expected for her to not be considered family, however my sisters and I are his blood children and they thought it was ok to leave us out as if we were not!!

I know you're wondering if there was a will and there was. When he died she produced an old will from before they ever got married. The will stated that if my father would die my stepmother would get the farm FEE SIMPLE, if she would die then the farm was to be split equally between their five children. Well, what FEE SIMPLE means is that she can do whatever she wants with the farm while she is still living. We went to a lawyer and there was nothing they could do about it!

I never put the word STEP in front of my sister, however the fact that she did that behind our backs is an indication she never valued that aspect therefore that's exactly what she became. I told her that I would always love her but that I could no longer have a relationship with her without having trust and roopoot.

They built a house on the farm and I'm really happy for them as I always thought they should have, however they could not comprehend the difference between being privileged and entitled.

PRIVILEGED; having special rights, rare opportunity to do something that brings you pleasure being connected to a noble person

ENTITLED; having THE right to certain benefits. Inherently deserving of privileges or special treatment being connected to a noble person.

I have forgiven her in my heart for myself because I was extremely angry about it for years. It's so hard to hang on to anger with someone you love so much.

I feel she was influenced by my stepmother's way of thinking that we were unworthy, ungrateful girls, when to be completely honest, we have never asked for anything from them but love and acceptance!

She should have done the noble thing even if it was standing up to her own mother, instead she ended up partaking in a very deceitful decision that could cause her bad karma for the rest of her life.

I will not allow myself to be fully in her life again unless she is willing to do the right thing by my sisters and I. It's not like we were estranged children that never cared for our father or came around him. We loved him very much. I can speak for myself that I had a great relationship with him and know in my heart that this is not what he would have wanted to see happen.

It goes back to me explaining how he never protected us girls from my stepmother's toxic ways. You don't have to hate someone just because they are toxic to you, it's bad for your soul and besides that I'm sure the guilt they carry is much more of a burden.

I just pray that someday they all end up doing right by us and give us a small piece of the property so we can build a family cabin to enjoy our memories where we all grew up at one time in our lives.

Or my book will be a number one seller and then I could offer them money for it! Wouldn't that be a noble thing to do, buy your own land back?

Perhaps a happy ending to all that hard emotional bullshit we had to go through most of our lives.

Or we can just appreciate my dads clothing items that we had to beg for and hug that teddy bear my sister had made from his shirts just a little tighter. **Perseverance!!!**

My point in telling this story is to inspire blended families to be more communicative, mindful, respectful and accepting of one another.

To trust, love and honor one another.

To have pride in yourself with the decisions you make when it affects someone else's well-being.

Parents and step-parents should protect their children from the thoughts of feeling unworthy!

OPEN MINDED

I try my hardest not to judge people for petty things or mostly nothing at all unless people are being unkind. I have a friend that back in the day she would make fun of everyone. I told her she better stop or karma would get her.

We played in a co-ed softball league together and during one game a ball slammed her right in the nose. She was bleeding bad so I quickly rushed her to the hospital. I went through every red light and I did manage to get her there safely!

They discovered she had broken her nose. She had to have surgery and they put this big white bandage on her nose. If we painted it red she would have looked like Rudolph! Guess what?? She got made fun of a lot! She then expressed to me that she heard my message and has been doing better on making fun of people.

Everyone is different and unique in their own way.

I find it interesting when people are different. How boring would life be if we were all the same. Walking around wearing the same clothes, hairstyle, carrying the same purse, driving the same car and agreeing on everything. That's what I would call weird if you ask me.

I really don't like to hear people say someone is weird or make fun of them just because they look or act different than them. I am probably most likely to judge myself the most, however I am working on that.

I actually came up with a new perspective for the word GOD (Gift-Of-Diversity). He created us all to be beautiful, different and unique for a reason.

HONEST

I'm a very honest person. You never have to guess what I am thinking. I'm pretty straightforward and authentic with people. I've had to learn to do more listening than talking and learn the difference between people asking for my advice/opinion or just needing an ear to just vent to.

I received my Life Coach Certificate, however I really haven't used it because I feel as if I'm not qualified to coach my family and friends. Perhaps they never really care what I think, they just want me to listen.

I absolutely hate it when people boss me around when I don't even ask their opinion so I TRY my best to respect that boundary for other people as well. It's a struggle sometimes…just sayin!

HELPFUL

So…apparently me being bossy was another thing a man I dated accused me of, so I came up with the fact that I am perhaps just aggressively helpful! We never like to face our own convictions. I took accountability for that one and tried to become more mindful of it and once again told myself to, "do better."

However, I will always help people. I'm not that person that only helps people that help me. That's not realistic. I don't typically need help doing things as I like to work on projects alone if I'm capable of the work. However, I'm very receptive and grateful when I do receive help in any way when I am in need.

If people aren't helping you it's most likely because you didn't ask or you didn't ask the right person. Or perhaps you're not very grateful, generous and too difficult to begin with. I do comprehend that, "you reap what you sow!"

MINDFUL
I honestly think that if you're in a relationship with anyone, not just a mate, you should stop and think before you do something or speak. Then ask yourself, "how would I want to be treated?" That's your answer.

Don't do or say something you would not appreciate done to yourself. Period. It's that simple.

I'm a thin person and I have been blessed with that my whole life. However, about ten years ago I started choking on my food and that was very scary. I couldn't eat any solid foods for almost a year without being afraid that I would choke to death! I got down to 101 pounds, when I would typically maintain between 115-120 pounds. I felt like a skeleton and was disgusted everytime I looked in the mirror. I had to learn to chew my food up until it became liquid before I would swallow it. I was starving because if you know me, I love to eat.

They discovered that I had a bad case of Acid Reflux which caused me to have Barrett's to the Esophagus. This could potentially lead to having the same condition my father died from which put me at high risk.

I had to have a surgery called the Linx Procedure. The Linx System is a small, flexible band of magnets enclosed in titanium beads and connected by titanium wires that they placed around my esophagus. It allows my esophagus to open and close properly after I eat.

It helped me tremendously, however I still suffer from eating like the average person and have a hard time maintaining a healthy weight. It's just as difficult for a thin person to feel like they are desirable as it is for an overweight person.

I would also like to express how rude it is to tell someone they are too skinny. Skinny people have feelings of insecurity as well as overweight people do. To tell a thin person they need to eat another cheeseburger (when they wish they could) is like telling an overweight person they should focus on saying, "NO" to that piece of chocolate cake they are always wanting to devour! Get my point?

I'm not too skinny because my doctors tell me I'm a perfect weight!

RULE BREAKER
I'm a disciplined person when it comes to my career, I've been self employed for twenty eight years so I've had to be. However, when I made a rule at the salon I was probably the first one to break it! I'm pretty free spirited, and never liked to micro-manage my girls. Freedom feels liberating!

I've never liked being tied down or caged up. I don't even like rules, never have. I've been a rule breaker since I can remember what the word meant. Shit, it took me about twenty seat belt fines and a truck constantly dinging at me before I would conform to that rule.

When I was in high school I would get caught smoking in the bathroom and get sent to ISS (In school suspension) While I was in ISS, even after writing, "I will not smoke on school property 500

times", I would get caught again for smoking in the bathroom! It's a wonder I'm not still in ISS!
I always try to pay the price gracefully. Well, most of the time. Being accountable has to come with grace. There is no such thing as perfection.

My mom tells me that as a child, I wasn't disrespectful to her when she grounded me, I would accept my punishment but after it was done I would still do whatever the hell I wanted to! That hasn't changed too much even as an adult.

TEMPERAMENTAL
My temper is another issue I've had to be humbled by. Boy oh boy has this and still does at times have to make me dig deep into reflecting. It has been my number one downfall, the most painful aspect of myself.

Now, it can be beneficial to my loved ones if I'm protecting them but if I'm holding them accountable for something then they definitely do not like the outcome. I can tell you that I have defended each and every person I know in my life a time or two if there is some valid reason that I should defend them. However, they most likely don't know this because I'm not a person who creates drama by telling people the opinion of others. Especially when it is unkind.

This is something I've always taught my daughters. Under no circumstances do you create drama with your friendships by partaking in senseless gossip!

When I was little I used to beat up my sister and the neighbor boy. My sister because that's what siblings do sometimes and the neighbor boy made me very aware that I do not like bullies!

While I was living in Virginia I had a friend that got mad at me because the boy she liked had a crush on me. I didn't like him except as a friend, perhaps he just thought I was cute and sweet, however she turned on me out of jealousy.

We were in the courtyard at our school when she came up to me accusing me of nonsense, pushed me and nearly knocked me down.

Now, she was six feet tall and probably twice my weight. I was 5'3, 115 lbs.

I thought to myself, "oh shit what do I do now?" "You can not let this girl push you around, be brave Tara!"

The memories of my childhood fights came back to me for a moment so that's when I went into that temper Tara mode and I kicked her ass right there in front of several students!

Everyone stood there in shock! They had no idea I was a little farm girl that could throw hay bales like a grown man. I heard people saying, "wow, I wouldn't want to mess with that girl!"

After that happened I became fearless of anyone and spent a great deal of my life not afraid to fight. I usually didn't start them, however I didn't take any shit from bullies or shitty people either!

One night I punched my uncle off of a barstool for calling my mom a bad name! Ya, not so proud of that as he is one of my favorite uncles. I was always protecting someone but I knew my behavior needed to change.

Violence is not a healthy trait to have.

I should have been a boxer, maybe that would have controlled my temper a bit better and I wouldn't have had so many hard lessons to learn. I can play the blame game my whole life and never want to change it or I can be aware of it, learn to control it and like myself a whole lot better by being accountable for it.

I have to say I get my temper honestly from my parents, dad as the ass kicker and my mom being extremely feisty in expressing her voice to be heard. I do know that we can't always blame our parents for our actions. They have had lessons to learn as well. There are times when we all need to tell ourselves that we need to do better.

Being a business owner for twenty eight years has also been a big attribute in helping me contain my temper.

CREATIVE
I am a Leo born in august so we tend to have what's called a monkey brain.

The "monkey brain" is a Buddhist term from centuries ago describing it as a mind filled with constant chatter, jumping from one thought to another and never at rest.

I have always struggled with this so that's when I discovered how artistic I was. When I couldn't shut my brain down I would work on an art piece. I like to repurpose things and turn them into beautiful art.

I feel like getting to know who you are and how your brain works is important for you to try different projects until one resonates with you.

When my dad passed I was so sad so I started creating bird baths made out of glass vases, bowls, plates and any little gadget that would make it look unique. I ended up making around fifty of them. It became a part of me so I kept creating all kinds of art using old items from the thrift store. It soothed my soul when I needed it the most.

I love going into my friends and families house and seeing my art pieces there for them to enjoy. I do it to keep my sanity and it brings me joy as well.

I have also realized that I am a creator not a maintainer. I like to move on to the next project and I have a hard time doing monotonous tasks. I like to pay it forward and hire people to do what I do not like to do.

HAPPY
I enjoy making people happy, however I do not wish to be dependent upon that for anyone. I try to encourage people to find happiness within themselves.

When you are single it's very important to maintain your own happiness because you are in your own company a lot.

Many people rely on others to find comfort and stability in their lives. It's important to lean on others, however true happiness lies within oneself. I've had to remind myself of this for many, many years until finally it resonated with me.

Do I get lonely sometimes? "Hell yeah, I'm human and we all need connection." However, most days I know that I have access to connection at any given moment rather through spiritual connection or simply just by picking up the phone to call upon someone who could fulfill that void.

I don't dwell in self pity for very long.

ADAPTIVE
I used to be extremely extroverted and always wanted to be around people. The older I get the more I value my alone time. It's my recharge time.

My job requires a lot of mental energy to help others feel good and look good. When you are in tune with the high energy of others it's important to take time for yourself.

It was after the Covid isolation I learned a side of me that I never realized before, I'm an Ambivert, which made me understand myself better.

So there are three different types. Introvert, Ambivert, and Extrovert. I discovered this when someone I was dating asked me to learn more about him being an Introvert.

Introvert; one who enjoys spending time with just one or two people, rather than large crowds. They feel more comfortable focusing on their inner thoughts and ideas, rather than what's happening externally. Prefer to have more alone time.

Ambivert; one whose personality is intermediate between both introvert and extrovert. Has friends of both types. Loves being with people but needs a recharge often. Requires alone time.

Extrovert; one that loves to be around people. Strong need to talk and socialize. Rarely requires alone time.

I recommend anyone to look more into it as it's very interesting and gets more in depth with the explanation of each type.

HOPEFUL
I enjoy having ME time and I require it for myself now without feeling guilty. I pay attention to my own needs while finding the time to nurture others.

I believe my hearing disability plays a part in requiring more alone time for myself. It gets very frustrating not being able to hear people correctly.

Comprehension hearing loss is what I have which has also affected my speech and unfortunately is not going to get better. I have formed a slight lisp which makes people ask me if I've been drinking sometimes. I do love to drink, however not typically all day long unless I'm on vacation or have a day off and my girlfriend wants to start drinking at noon on a Monday!

Hearing aids help in certain situations but mostly they are of equal frustration. Sometimes it's funny what I think people say, however when people act as if I'm unintelligent, that is when it can become hurtful. It's also frustrating when people mumble or talk extremely loud when it's only necessary to raise your voice just a little higher.

It's an insecurity issue for me that I have had to work on and still do. This is something that people could become more mindful of as well.

DEDICATED
I will always have a dog in my life especially now that I'm eligible for a service dog booausc of my

hearing disability. They bring me such joy and fill any void of loneliness.

As a child, we were never allowed to have indoor pets so when I became a dog mom for the first time it was a challenge. I didn't realize how much work you have to put into having a good dog. It's kind of like being a parent but they can't talk back. Yes they are work and can be a hassle sometimes but the benefits out rule the cons for sure.

I'm not certain I could handle being single as well as I do without having a dog to come home to every day.

Dogs are great for companionship, depression, anxiety, loyalty, loneliness, exercise and giving you a purpose along with feeling safe.

ADDICTIVE
The thing I'm hardest on myself the most is the fact that I smoke cigarettes. I know I can quit if I really put my mind to it, however it's been my biggest challenge.

When I was young, I think maybe five years old, my mom caught me smoking in the closet. She made me smoke until I was sick. As a mother we never know what the right punishment should be so I don't judge her for that but it obviously didn't work.

I feel as if I've been addicted my whole life.

My mom didn't smoke while she was pregnant with my older sister, she smoked a little with my middle sister and with me she was a full-blown smoker. My older sister never smoked, my middle sister can smoke one cigarette a day and I have been addicted to smoking for many years. Actually since I was 14. I'm not saying that's why but the theory is interesting.

I'm hopeful someday I will kick the habit. It's definitely very frowned upon these days. I like to smoke, but then I don't like to smoke. Always so conflicted and disappointed when I try to quit. That's the hard part. My dad quit for six months and I was so proud of him. Then one day he started smoking again, and I asked him why? He said, "Tara, I just didn't feel like myself without smoking."

It does scare me a lot because he died a couple of years later from cancer at sixty two years old.

My mom quit twenty years ago and I'm so proud of her. She doesn't like me to smoke and is mostly supportive and says I'll quit when I'm ready. She even offered me $1000 if I quit for a year. I must be crazy not to do this! I know it's bad for me, however If one more ex-smoker tells me I need to quit….. That's just so not cool and judgemental! I know this and would like to say, "Mind your business but thanks for caring!"

OPTIMISTIC
What I like the most about who I am is that I find the positive aspect before the negative and I have taken many risks while encouraging people to do the same because of this mindset.

On the flip side I feel I have also had issues with people in my life because of this, however I believe it is because they are not of the same mindset nor do they want to be. They want me to validate their negative views and join in on some sort of pity party. Or they want me to agree with them while having a gossip session about someone I care about but typically I prefer to defend and try to get them to see another side. A lot of times it turns into me defending myself for taking a stance for the greater good with closed minded people. You know, misery loves company!

At times I feel like an outcast from this trait. Like I don't fit in because I'm so happy and usually can see the brighter side. I feel as if I get on people's nerves if I am too positive. It can make me feel sad and frustrated at times, however I understand that some people just don't try to be any different. They can't comprehend the fact that we all have the capability to change our mindset at any given moment.

Some of the risks I've taken have worked out and some have not. I just focus on the ones that have and the people who value that about me. I know why I'm here, to dream without fear.

FRUGAL
I am a thrifter. I love finding good deals at a thrift store. I love spending the day with my momma and sisters going to every thrift store we can find and compare our magical items. We like saving money on bougie things.

I'm a girl that will spend more money on my flower beds than any clothing item or purse. That's my beauty.

VERSATILE
I like to get dressed up and look pretty to go out and dance the night away, but I can also ride a quad like a badass and enjoy getting muddy. My flower beds are my therapy as well. I love to be outside enjoying nature and soaking up some

sunshine. That's the farm girl in me that will never go away

DETERMINED
The one part of me that I haven't decided how I feel about yet is that I'm very competitive and refuse to give up.

My dads nickname for me was PITA (Pain in the ass). I believe that was because I do not like to take NO for an answer!

 I never know when to give up on certain people or challenges to the point that it causes me to become emotionally and physically drained. I've always been the type to never give up until I feel confident that I have given it my ALL without a shadow of any doubt!

This next journey of mine will leave you wondering as well…

"Don't ever give someone the ammunition to tell you who you are….if YOU know who you are there will be no reason to contest such foolishness!"

-Tara Flaherty-

Feeling unconditional love (Pablo)

It was a crisp Thursday night in May, Cinco de Mayo day. I went out for the first time in a long time on a weekday. My friend asked me to join them and I accepted the invite. We went to a local bar that was having karaoke. We were having a nice time having some girl time and drinks. However, I can't sing so no way was I getting up there and making a fool of myself!

A song came on that I love and a handsome man and a woman were singing. I was mesmerized by his voice and then when I looked at him I couldn't stop staring at him because he was so hot! He had a ball cap on but it appeared that his hair was black, brown eyes and his body was so sexy and built.

The way he sang was so beautiful. He put so much energy into the song by Meat Loaf, "Two Out of Three Ain't Bad." I just melted listening and watching him, I got the tingle! I said to myself, "I hope that is his sister and not a girlfriend." I leaned over to my friend and told her that I thought he was cute and ironically she knew him, his name is Pablo and yes it was his sister.

She went over to talk to him after they sang and she invited him to our table. I was so nervous and couldn't quit tingling. Girls know what the tingle means. We talked a lot and then he asked me to dance. I hoped he was into me as much as I was him.

The night was coming to an end at the bar so he asked if he could give me a ride home. Of course I couldn't resist, however that wasn't something I would typically do at that point in my life but I still couldn't resist the tingle.

We pulled into my driveway, my daughters were home so I didn't ask him to come inside because I never did that kind of thing when my girls were there. I tried to set a good example for them when I could.

There was such an intense connection with him that made me feel so intrigued. When he kissed me for the first time it was like my whole body became so light weight. It was so passionate that we couldn't stop.

Right in my driveway at 2:30 in the morning, I felt my whole body go numb as if I was in another world. I felt as if my soul connected with his and it was so amazing. I had sex in his car, in my driveway for the first time and I couldn't wait to do it again!

All week long I couldn't stop thinking about that amazing night. I had told him that night, "this was just a one night stand!" He said, "no, it was a first night stand!" We did not exchange numbers! Why in the hell did I say that? I didn't want it to be a one night stand! He was amazing.

The next Thursday night couldn't come soon enough. I called my friend this time to see if they were going out again. I just had to see him again!

We walked in and the bar was busy as usual. I scanned the place out but I didn't see him. All of the sudden out of my peripheral vision I saw a hot Mexican walking beside me. I was too scared to look. I saw him go to my friend and have a conversation. I could see him get his phone out and then all of the sudden I got a text saying it's Pablo and asked where I was. Apparently my friend gave him my number.

I was watching them and suddenly he started to come towards me. I was so nervous but I didn't let that be known. He came over and hugged me, I was tingling all over again.

I was so happy and we couldn't keep our hands off of eachother.

I had a great night dancing and watching him sing again.

So guess what happens next? Sex in my driveway in his car again! Oh my it was another night to remember. I slept well but he had to sleep in his car because I wouldn't let him stay with me as my girls were there again.

The next day I text him, "want to have a beer and sex in bed?" It was a definite, "hell yes" response! He came over and we were having a wonderful time until my sis called and said they were taking my dad to the ER. He had just been diagnosed with esophageal cancer, had pneumonia and was struggling to breathe. We cut the night short and I went to see my dad.

It had been two weeks since I last heard from Pablo so I finally texted him. He said he had been struggling because in the meantime he had lost his step dad. I felt bad for him as I was also facing emotional issues with my dad being sick as well.

We had a lot of fun getting to know each other. I didn't want to be really pushy but I loved being with him. I loved to hear him sing so we went to karaoke a lot.

My family, friends and I planned a benefit for my dad so he could seek extra holistic medical care for his cancer so Pablo helped me write a song for him to play at the benefit. My girlfriend sang the song and he played the guitar. It was absolutely beautiful. I wish someday it could be played on the radio.

They really sounded amazing together!

The song goes like this:

To Me your Everything

Just driving the day away,
sitting on your lap and you would say,
"keep her straight don't look away,"
teaching me how to bail the hay.

Oh I remember the day,
The day that Eddie went away,
"Times were tough" you would say,
I know it had to be that way.

Chorus:
To me your everything,

Everything a man should be,
Stubborn and strong for me,
Grumpy occasionally….
Papa, your never wrong to me,
Abrasive enough to make me see,
You're everything a man should be.

To me you are not less than,
I know your doing all that you can,
As I see you facing your fears,
Holding back all your tears.
Courage and strength from above,
All I need is your love.

To me your everything,
Everything a man should be,
Stubborn and strong for me,
Grumpy occasionally….
Papa, your never wrong to me,
Abrasive enough to make me see,
You're everything a man should be.

Chorus again.

Just driving the day away,
Sittin' on your lap and you would say,
"Keeper straight, don't look away,"
Teaching me how to bail the hay.

Pablo would always be amazing one minute and then not so much the next. When my dad passed away after dating for nearly a year he made no effort to come to the funeral and that really broke my heart and people judged him for that. I forgave him because that's who I am and I understood him more than he knew I did as he was an introvert. It always hurts me to think about it, however in his defense he started a new job then and didn't have time off accumulated yet.

Also in his defense, I had told him the night my dad passed that I needed him. When I got home he was there waiting for me along with several friends. As I appreciated my friends caring about me, it was Pablo I wanted and needed the most at that moment but I didn't have the courage to tell my friends.

Pablo left that night so I could be with my friends and I do regret that. He always thought I put my friends before him. I got accused of that a lot in my past relationships.

We ended up having an intense physical, soulful connection but a horrible communicable connection. We couldn't talk about anything important and always had to guess what each other was thinking and feeling.

When we first met he told me he was divorced. I started to notice things that didn't add up so I asked him a couple months later and he admitted that his divorce wasn't final yet. He claimed that he lied because he didn't think I would talk to him if he was still married. I'm not that type of woman and I also know that people need to heal after a divorce so he's probably right about that one. I forgave him but I also realized my trust issues started with him from that long ago.

Almost two years went by and we still couldn't connect on that level so I broke up with him hoping that he would miss me... Well during that time he met another woman instead. I was just devastated! She was so different from me.

He went several years going back and forth between the two of us. I couldn't understand why he would always choose her. He told me later that it wasn't ever because he cared for her more, however they came from a similar upbringing and he felt that she understood him better.

As time went by I realized she was just a victim of his dysfunctional, unemotional, damaged by lack of trust for women and afraid to be vulnerable as well as I was.

I thought I was a breath of fresh air for him after the things I heard he went through with his ex-wife. I was independent, strong, compassionate and really thought I had my shit together.

When we first started to date I told him I didn't need a man. I guess I left out the fact that I wanted a man, especially him. Wouldn't it feel better to be wanted rather than needed? Apparently he wasn't ready to be wanted.

Pablo went through a dysfunctional childhood where he had to fend for himself at a very young age. He also had a challenging marriage for almost twenty years that he was used to being needed. That was his normal.

I can remember the day I fell in love with Pablo like it was yesterday.

We were at his sisters where Pablo was staying at the time and that's where I met his mom. She was a short little Mexican lady who was so cute and sweet. Pablo told me all the hardship that he had gone through as a child so it was so sweet when I saw him kiss her on the top of her head and tell her he loved her. My dad used to do that with me so I just melted when I saw him do that.

He was a man who held no resentment, well at least not on the surface. I fell instantly in love with him.

I loved that Pablo held nobody accountable in rebuilding his life. He was a man on a mission, to be free from the feeling of not having enough.

I have watched Pablo grow in an unimaginable way for what he had gone through. I have so much respect for this man, however that caused me a lot of pain for almost twelve years because I allowed him to hurt me. I know he didn't deliberately mean it, he just gained so much independence and freedom that I feel he will never want to commit again until it's too late for me.

I tried to move on so many times, I even got engaged briefly to a man that I had dated for a short time in my early twenties. At first this man made me feel like I could move forward from this unconditional, soulful love. He was a great guy. A very fun, loving, generous, loyal person that would do anything for me, however he had issues as well.

He would sometimes drink too many shots that made him say really mean things to me. I gave him lots of warnings before he tapped into Temperamental Tara, "No way was I living like that!"

To be honest, I also couldn't forget the feeling of the unconditional love I felt for another man.

Once again I became available to Pablo.

This has been years of on-again, off-again beautiful intimacy and a great time together. I think eight months is the longest we have gone without at least seeing each other even if it were just for one night or to have a beer and catch up on our lives. I always felt as if I would never find someone and feel the way I did for Pablo....

Why?

Is this going to go on forever?

Will I ever have this connection with someone else again?

After the pandemic in 2020 we got together more frequently and started to communicate on a better level.

The next January, we vowed that we would try to make it work again. So for six months I went to his house every weekend. I was so excited when Friday came because I knew we were going to have a great time. It was like watching two teenagers if you were there.

I packed up everything I needed every weekend and took my dogs there and we fell in love all over again. We cooked together, worked on projects at his house and made his basement into our playroom. We would Play darts, jam to music, dance and sing together or just chill and watch movies.

We would drink a lot of tequila at times which made him become very vulnerable with his emotions. He would cry about things from his past, his family and how he wished he could be different towards me. He always claimed to be a lost cause. I never wanted to believe that. I felt so connected and always felt deep empathy for him. I loved every minute of our time together. We couldn't get enough of each other!

We even went to Key West, Florida with my family and had a wonderful time. Everything was going great besides that I wished I could see him more through the week, however our schedules didn't allow that to happen. I also wished that we would start moving towards some kind of committed future together.

In June we went to my camper at the lake in Marblehead. I wasn't feeling well that day, most likely from having too much fun the night before. We were sitting by the pool and I started to feel extremely weak and lightheaded. I thought I was just hungry and getting too hot. We headed back to the camper and I could barely walk.

Pablo went to get the truck and when he got back he found me sitting on a golf cart unresponsive. I woke up to people all around me and the squad was there. I fell out again! It was very scary! They put me in the squad and took me to the hospital. My blood pressure was 70/49. I was extremely dehydrated. I had told Pablo to stay at the camper because he had been drinking and I didn't want him to drive. I knew he wouldn't do well at the hospital.

When I got back he just started to cry and told me how much he loved me and couldn't lose me. It felt so good to hear him say that! I thought for some reason there was going to be something good that would come out of my near death experience. We made love and cuddled all night.

When we woke up I thought things would be different, perhaps we would start planning our life together. Absolute opposite! He was back to his distant sober self. I couldn't believe it! Why? What is this man thinking? Is he that scared of love? Or just simply the most uncommittable, afraid to be vulnerable while being sober man that I've ever met?

That next week he shut me out completely! Came up with every excuse to not want to be with me. I was so heartbroken. I tried to stay away from him for three months with everything I had while my heart ached for him. I cried myself to sleep for many nights. I finally pulled it together and started to date someone else. That lasted a whole three weeks!

Pablo started to reach out again so we started the whole DAMN process over AGAIN!

I became numb to the idea that we were ever going to commit to each other and decided to just enjoy the time I had with him. It was like an addiction I couldn't say no to.

I would go for me, not him. I got something out of it. I was no longer sad when I left the next day. I stopped planning out our future in my head and just accepted what we had in the moment. I stopped always trying to see him.

I knew he loved me as much as he could love any woman but there was no way we had a future together anytime soon.

Best thing I could hope for is when we get old we would be that cute little couple, holding hands and doting over each other until our lives come to an end.

In the meantime I didn't want to date anyone else, however I did have some fun as a cougar(jaguar) while we were apart. Having a boy toy would be safe with my emotions. When you are a sexual person living the single life, you have to resort to possibly being a "slut", finding someone new or going back to the familiar with an ex which is typically too much drama. I played it safe with a boy toy, no commitment, thoughts of any expectations or becoming emotionally attached!

This idea is also a great ego boost for a fifty one year old woman going through menopause, watching her body deplete its muscles and elasticity. It is not the walk of "shame", it's the walk of "fame!" You feel liberated in the self-esteem department. A much younger man is still attracted to me? Wow, I still got it going on!

Pablo who??

Oh...he did not like that idea at all, however even jealousy could not awaken him to see the value of what we had. I know he had been seeing other women as well but he was not as honest about it. It made me feel crazy and realized that I have got to get my shit together!

I finally accepted that the one thing I got out of this relationship is that I learned what true unconditional love feels like. It hurts so bad but at least I have finally felt it. I will forever be grateful for that.

I have hurt a lot of men in my past and always felt that if I would have ever known the feeling of unconditional love then why could I have walked away so easily?

I thought I felt it with my high school love as it took me years to stop thinking of him.

I thought I felt it with my ex-husband but if I had then why was it so easy for me to get a divorce?

When I met Pablo it was different for me. It was a soul connection from the beginning that made my whole body feel at peace when we were together. I truly loved him, not just for what he could be for me but for what I could be for him as well.

I made more excuses for him than any man I have ever known. I had true empathy for him and his past life. I didn't care.

I loved him for all the things he did right, not for all the things he did wrong.

I was proud of the man he was, not for the man that I nor anyone else wanted him to be.

I realize that I will never free myself from this type of relationship if I don't start to value myself and love ME unconditionally. That is my new mission.

Writing this book and reading this dysfunction has become the start of a healing process for me in many aspects.

Another excuse Pablo gave that he couldn't commit to me was because I was too positive and expected people to be happy all the time. That's when I finally got the strength to walk away again.

I was allowing someone with emotional issues to jeopardize my self worth. I will never let someone degrade my God given gift because he felt intimidated by it or perhaps has low self worth issues causing him to convince himself that we weren't good together. Regardless, I couldn't take the constant excuses anymore no matter how much love I felt for him.

I do know that he loves me as much as he can love a woman, he just can not commit, perhaps because of the guarded brick wall he has put up from his past.

To speak honestly about myself and my accountability to this relationship, it could be possible that I don't feel comfortable with commitment any more than he does and that could be why we have stayed in phase one of our relationship for so long.

If this would be correct then I have some healing to do from my past traumas within myself as well.

However, I don't like hurting people from this mindset. That's the difference!

"Letting go is not giving up, it's allowing yourself to grow from the pain and become open to the possibility to live your best life with or without someone."

"Love is not a feeling of intelligence, it's fuel for strength."

"Do not hate yourself for being in love, hate the idea of never being capable of knowing what it feels like.
-Tara Flaherty-

*"To be brave is to love
Someone unconditionally,
Without expecting
Anything in return."*
-Madonna-

Loving myself

I did some research on this and I found it very interesting and fun while discovering who I am and learning to love myself as well as areas I could focus on to live my best life.

Getting up everyday and looking your best is a start. Paying attention to the beauty of myself, not the flaws. Wrinkles are wise lines and happen to every beautiful soul. Gray hair can be colored but it still happens gracefully.

I looked at my body totally naked in the mirror and pointed out the beautiful aspects of it, not the aging areas of it. I told myself all the things I loved about myself, not the things other people view me as or don't appreciate because perhaps they may not feel good about themselves.

I decided to pay attention to the people who care about me for all the wonderful things that I am, what I do to lift others up, not just what I can do or be for them.

There will always be someone that wants you on the lowest altitude with them. However, there will always be someone cheering you on as they pave a path for you to rise to the highest altitude as well.

"Learning and growing in this great big universe".

I listed some habits of an unhappy and happy person based on research and added some stuff to it as well. I made it into a quiz for myself.

The habits do not mean you're a certain type of person all the time, it's just things we do while we are unhappy or happy.

I would say if you score very high on either perspective then that should tell you where you are on the happiness scale. Just something to bring to the journey of finding myself. That was kind of fun yet holding me accountable.

I turned on one of my favorite songs, "man in the mirror" and I answered all of them as truthfully as I could with yes, no, or could do better.

Take the test with me. It's fun but also be honest with yourself.

"Normal could possibly mean you're doing ordinary things, abnormal could possibly make you do extraordinary things."

Habits of unhappy people

- Let past/future thoughts overwhelm them
- Compare themselves to others
- Care about opinions of others
- Get sucked in by negatives of life
- Over complicating life
- Critize others
- Do things only for personal gain/selfish
- Blame others
- Pick fights with others
- Don't celebrate
- Quit often/ lack of goals
- Very controlling
- Gossip and moan
- Fill a void with things
- Wanting perfection
- Hang out with negative people
- Distrusting of strangers
- Hold grudges
- No gratitude
- Sweep serious issues under the rug
- Don't think they can learn new things
- Worry over money regardless their wealth
- Make everything about them
- Jump to conclusions
- Poor diet choices

My score was Yes=0 No=17 Could do better=8

Please understand that if you are doing some of these habits it doesn't necessarily mean you are an unhappy person all the time but perhaps you are unhappy at that moment while doing them.

For example, I don't typically jump to conclusions but when I'm feeling unhappy with someone or myself I let that narrator in my head convince me of all sorts of different scenarios.

When I'm feeling unhappy I may go shopping and buy too many things to try to lift me up. I normally hate shopping and spending money on myself.

When I gossip and moan I typically have to be going through something uncomfortable with someone or don't feel well but as a rule I don't just sit around and gossip or moan about people and my life in general. That usually bothers me.

This is just something for us to guide ourselves, so don't beat yourself up if you scored too high. Just notice it and do better, that's what I do.

Habits of happy people

- Grateful, not hateful
- Spend quality time with loved ones
- Mindful of others
- Set boundaries with others
- Compliment others
- Choose friends wisely
- Eat right
- Sleep well
- Meditate
- Masterbate
- Exercise
- Lean on loved ones
- Drink more water
- Journal
- Higher expectations of self
- Smile
- Don't judge others
- Self-care
- Take time alone
- Take a vacation
- Have a hobby
- Make their bed
- Take pride in their personal space
- Generosity/ serving
- Like to Learn something new
- Good hygiene

My score was Yes=18 No=1 Could do better=7

So, I scored higher on the happy scale but that doesn't mean I don't have some reflection to do within myself.

You see people believe that they can't change or that other people can't change but this is absolutely not true. Sometimes it doesn't have to be, "it is what it is."

If you stay the same person you've always been then you're not growing which means you're possibly not living to the fullest version of yourself.

Aspire to live your best life rather than to just get by, or fear you're not really living much of a life at all?

That's unacceptable for my life! I want to do my best, I want to be the happiest version of myself!

Yes, I said the word masturbation!

This is a book written by a single woman. Nobody wants to talk about the benefits of this because it's an awkward subject but it shouldn't be. Orgasm is a natural human need,

I don't know how married people can tell me they don't have sex anymore and also think masturbation is dirty! I can't help but wonder if maybe they have never had an orgasm? I personally feel withholding sex from each other without a medical or physical/mental reason should be considered some sort of abuse. I'm sorry but I feel as if that's not fair to your partner if they still want or need it.

You should not have to beg for sex!

To be honest I feel that could be why people are not faithful in their relationships. Not that I support that behavior, however it should be communicated.

I can speak for ladies though, women can not have sex with a man if they are mean to them. We are emotional when it comes to sex. We have to feel sexy, desired and valued. You shouldn't call your partner bad names, treat them with disrespect and then expect her/him to jump into bed with you! Do better!

masturbation is good for all of these reasons.

Better sleep
Stress reliever/ anxiety
Heart health

Healthy vagina
Pain reducer
Expanded pleasure
Bladder control
Sexual issues
Boost your sexual desires for you and your partner

My sis, who is an ER nurse, said, "Use it or lose it!" That applies to both men and women.

Taking pride in your personal space is a big one as well. Your bedroom should be the most peaceful room in your house. It's what you wake up to every morning so it should bring you happiness and peacefulness when you go to sleep at night. No mess. No clutter. Your sanctuary. Just my perspective. It works for me.

Now I have to admit I did not make my bed for years. I Just didn't see the point if I were going to just mess it up again anyways.

 It wasn't until a few years ago that I was staying in a cabin with my girlfriends and I came across this little book called, "Make Your Bed" by William H. McRaven. They made fun of me because I couldn't stop reading it. It made a lot of sense to me! It's the first thing you can start your day off with accomplishing something good or… anything at all.

So after I read that book I started making my bed everyday! I love the way my bedroom looks when I'm done. I take pride in it now.

Loving yourself is protecting yourself. Your feelings matter. I have learned to enjoy myself, date myself for say. Not be afraid of my own company.

I watch tv shows that make me happy and not feel bad about something or the way the news can portray that this is a horrible life we live in.

Now, don't get me wrong, I do have a stance in my beliefs, however I don't make it my everyday topic that's up for discussion, especially if there is not a damn thing I can do to fix it!

I like to hang out with people that I can laugh with or have a good deep conversation with like minded people about how mysterious life can be. I do not care what someone looks like, what they wear or even how they express themselves. I only care about the integrity of that person and how they treat me and other living beings.

I love my life because of the blessings I have been receptive to and the sacrifices I have been willing to make by being vulnerable.

I don't focus on what I don't have or what I am not.

I notice what people do, not what they don't do.

I love me now, flaws and all.

I stopped striving so much and learned to feel alive.

Strive-thrive-feel alive.

"You don't have to be great to get started, but you have to get started to be great."
Quote by Less Brown. Another great mentor of mine.

It takes work to maintain happiness and self worth. I don't deserve this kind of life anymore than you reading this book. I just desire it for myself. I try not to say, "I hope to". I say, "I intend to" or "I will", especially when it's in my hands to get accomplished. I have more to add to this in the chapter on my journey to true vulnerability. It saved me and helped me to learn to love myself.

You yourself, as much as anybody in the entire universe, deserve your love and affection!

When you see yourself clearly,
With eyes full of love and acceptance,
You hold space for others
To meet you at your highest self.
-Karly Ryan-

My daily prayer

Thank you for me and my health.
Thank you for my family
Thank you for My most precious blessings, my beautiful daughters.
Thank you for my friends.
Thank you for my pets.
Thank you for my generous clients, prosperous salon and wonderful girls.
Thank you for my home, my beautiful sanctuary.
Thank you for all the abundance you give me in my life and guiding me to be receptive to it.
All is well. Amen.

"Acknowledging the good that you already have in your life, is the foundation for all abundance."
-Eckhart Tolle-

To Live by Intention

To feel peace
Is to be
Exactly who
You are
With
Acceptance,
Without
Contradiction,
Without
Judgement,
Without doubt.
Just pure love.

- Tara Flaherty-

Wayne Dyer is one of my most respected mentors. I have been reading his books and listening to his audios for years. I never got the chance to meet him but he impacted my life more than he will ever know. He's easy to listen to and his sweet demeanor made a lot of sense to me on the seven faces of intention that God created us to be. We are all given this intention at birth so it is up to us to maintain it throughout our lives.

The 7 faces of intention-Wayne Dyer-

To be creative- everyone has a creative side to them rather it be through art, music, writing, solving problems or simply being entertaining.

To be kind- we can all be kind just by being helpful, listening to someone in need or simply smiling and holding a door open for someone.

To be beautiful- having beauty is possessing qualities that give great pleasure or satisfaction to see. Delighting the senses or mind. Enhancing your true self.

To be loving- to feel or show true care and empathy for others. It's the highest vibrational energy to god.

To expand our lives- to not fear our dreams. Anything is possible if you desire it for your life. We all have the same god given rights.

To live in abundance- there will always be enough for everyone. Plentifulness of the good things in life. Prosperity with gratitude.

To be receptive- willingness to be acceptive or consider suggestions or new ideas. Ready and willing to receive your gifts from God and anyone who wants to be generous to you as well. You ask, you shall receive.

"Our Intention
Creates our reality."
-Wayne Dyer-

I wanted to go somewhere special to write my book. I wasn't rich but I believed in myself and my intentions were clear. I made a plan and expected nothing less for myself.

Everything fell into place exactly as I wished for. There were a few bumps in the road but I just kept a clear vision and stayed on the route I was supposed to follow while having no fear.

"Investing in yourself is fearless vulnerability, feeling liberated without doubting your ability!"

Beyond success

Fifteen years ago I received my instructors license in my profession and designed a motivational workshop to help inspire people to go beyond their potential and truly spread their wings and not limit their dreams and aspirations.

I never did anything with it because I have always been uncomfortable talking in front of people, especially after I developed a lisp from my hearing loss. It has always been my fear, however I'm hopeful someday I can overcome those limitations I put on myself.

I would like to share my perspective of the fifteen principles that I believe it takes to become successful in life. When I decided to invest in myself to take an entire month off, go somewhere beautiful and write my book, I used these principles to make it happen for me. I wasn't rich, I just believed in myself.

Also, I did not change one word of these principles that I wrote fifteen years ago. They remain the same and I still wholeheartedly believe every word.

1. To find your purpose- intention

Who are you and what do you want to do with your life? What inspires you? What are your dreams, and how can you work towards making them happen? Definite of purpose is the starting point towards every achievement. Make a plan of action and move towards making your life what you want it to be. You'll get exactly and only what you ask for. Your intentions are to be or not to be. We all have a destination, however it is our choice as to how to get there. Don't be a ship at sea without a rudder, powerless with no sense of direction!

2.To create-visualize,anything is possible

The creative mind can visualize the finished product. To think out of the box and believe that anything is possible. Everyone has a creative mind if you want to tap into it. Everything in this world was created by thought and put into existence from a creative mind. Have you ever invented something in your mind and then seen it be created by someone else? The greatest inventors believed in meditation to help clear their minds from stress and too much mental commotion.

3. To use your resources- build an alliance

When you figure out who you are and what you want to be you must build an alliance and use your resources to help you achieve your goals. No man can accomplish their dreams alone. Talk about what you want to do with your life and the right people will be there to help mastermind it. Whether it be a loan officer to help you get started, a client to perform a service on or just a friend to help with support. Not one person can become successful without the help from others. Every step of our lives has purpose. We just have to figure out why people are put into our life, sometimes for a reason or a season, for the meantime or a lifetime.

4. To have faith- believe in yourself.

Faith is the confident belief or trust in the truth or worthiness of a person, idea or thing. It is the power of thought. "Whatever the mind can conceive and believe, the mind can achieve"(Napoleon Hill). If you don't believe in yourself then nobody else will. Our thoughts can control our destiny. Faith can move mountains, doubt can create them. Let go of all fear. Faith is worth far more than how educated you might be… And it's free.

5. To motivate- give incentive and encouragement

When you make a plan of action you must bring it into motion. Don't sit around and think about what you're going to do, just do it! Completion is the power of action. Take personal initiative to bring your thoughts into action and encourage others to join in with the incentive to move towards success. You never know the outcome of something until you put forth the effort and get motivated.

6. To have a positive mental attitude -optimistic

A positive attitude is one of life's most riches... It is our attitude that creates our success. Anything worthwhile begins with optimism. Keep your mind on the things you want and off the things you don't want. If you think you are sick you will be, if you think your day is bad it will get worse. If you think you can accomplish your dreams, you will. Anything is possible. Is your life half over or do you have half your life yet to live? Do you quack like a duck or soar like an eagle?

7. To have enthusiasm -inspire with excitement

Enthusiasm is the most contagious of all emotions. Whatever you do or say, excitement will draw people to you for inspiration. It is an emotion that will never be found in an ailing body. You will never experience your full potential without being enthusiastic about what you are doing. Everyday people want to be inspired, why couldn't it be from you?

8. To concentrate-pay attention to now

If you were more concerned with what happened yesterday or what will be tomorrow then you will miss out on what is happening right here in the now. When our minds wander off we could be missing a valuable link to what might be of service to us by not paying attention. Listening to others is the best quality to have. Concentration is the power of production. Living in the now is the most peaceful place to be.

9. To be receptive- be open minded

Be willing to be open to new ideas or perceptions of others. Don't be afraid to let someone else in on your ideas. Two minds are stronger than one. Except help and learn to delegate tasks that are too large to do by yourself. Do not judge someone else because we are all different and have our own vision of how we want things to be.

10. To be a team player- willing to work together

Teamwork is sharing a responsibility or task with others to reach a common goal. Leaders set the pace and work well together to accomplish success. A team player will recognize the efforts of others and will appreciate it. They are problem solvers not creators. They will never stop participating just because others refuse to.

11. To be resilient -overcome adversity

The ability to overcome adversity is to be able to accept a challenge that may not have been in your plan. To never give up on what you have worked so hard for. When one plan falls through you try another. You will not be defeated unless you accept it as such. Emotional gain is more important than material gain. Sometimes when we think we have failed, it's only a temporary detour, a new direction for something bigger and better.

12. To serve-go above and beyond

When you get where you want to be you must never take it for granted. Success is precious and can be taken from you if you don't respect it. You didn't get there alone, so you must continue to serve the people who admire your accomplishments. Go the extra mile to continue to grow. Continue to give back even if you get nothing in return. Doing something for free is a reward to your soul. It keeps you gracious with a great peace of mind. The most successful people are always willing to go above and beyond.

13. To Please-be kind, compassionate and patient

A happy person with good energy is so pleasurable to be around. Just because you are having a bad day doesn't give you the right to ruin someone else's day. The way you present yourself is exactly what you will get back. Your personality is what you transmit to the world. Be kind, compassionate and patient, it is what we long for in ourselves and in others. It's the most important thing people will remember about you.

14. To be disciplined - break bad habits

You have to be willing to do the tasks that are required of you in order for your plan to become successful. You can't write a book without taking the time to buy paper and type. You can't be at work on time without getting up on time. You can't provide a service and never be there. You can't have children and expect them to raise themselves. Discipline is the power of dedication which is the fuel for success. Form new habits that will serve you in your journey.

15. To balance- ability to maintain health and wealth

Balance is the ability to maintain health and wealth. It is the key to life's riches of health, happiness and peace of mind. When you do not balance your life you become sick and stressed out, which ultimately brings you to some sort of failure. For the successful person a day should be divided as such: eight hours for sleep, eight hours for work, and eight hours for normal tasks and play. A young happy, healthy heart ages gracefully. Stress will make you sick and old before your time. Budget your money as well and always know your balance in the bank! Success has little to do with how much money you make or how big your house is. Are you happy, healthy and do you feel joy with who you are and what your purpose is?

> *"Success is not final,*
> *Failure is not fatal,*
> *It is the courage to continue*
> *That counts."*
>
> -WINSTON S. CHURCHILL-

Journey to true vulnerability

Just a girl and her dog

So the day has finally come for my Puerto Rico trip to come here to finish writing my book with my dog Zoie. I wanted to go somewhere different to experience their way of living. Somewhere warm, peaceful and humbling so that I could better appreciate my own life.

Zoie is my amazing Labradoodle. She is not only my service dog, she is my best furry friend. Sometimes I feel as if she is part human by the way she is so attentive and docile. She is truly a princess dog. She loves everyone and has this personality that makes everyone want a dog just like her. I told her when she was a puppy that "everyone deserves love." I really think she understood that message and if you know Zoie you would have to agree with me. She is truly one of a kind!

I feel my life is wonderful, however I needed some serious R&R. I'm always busy doing something and I need to feel that peace that I've always desired to be able to write to my fullest potential with no distractions. However…..my family is very protective of me so my sisters invited themselves for the first week to get me there safely. Sibling love is something we will always have between the three of us!

The first day of travel was definitely a challenge in getting there without frustration!

I love to travel and flying is my preferred way to get somewhere, however I am typically a light packer so going somewhere for a whole month with my dog was not going to be an easy task to pack light!

I took a big suitcase and a small one. The big one ended up being overweight and cost me $100 extra to check it. Then my small suitcase had all of my liquid stuff in it so I had to check it in as well for $45. My sister's suitcase was also overweight. Another $100.

The lady at the desk had zero patience and didn't even give us time to decide what to do about it. That ended up costing $270 at 4:30 AM without having much coffee!

My sister said in a very quiet voice, "a little patience would be nice!" Needless to say I wanted to go "Temperamental Tara" on her but I remained in check with my emotions. I told her that she had zero patience and she basically threw a temper tantrum and told me that I hurt her feelings by telling her that she was impatient.

She was the manager so that was absolutely unacceptable!

That's the typical response of someone who just wants their behavior to be dismissed and coddled so that they can go about their day and not have to be accountable.

I continued on and just tried to send her good vibes and was proud of myself for not losing my shit like I most likely would have done in the past.

It was the first plane ride for Zoie and she did amazing. Couldn't have been more proud of her as I knew and visualized her to be. My sis also brought her dog Moose and it was his first plane ride as well at fourteen years old. He also did amazing!

We arrived in Puerto Rico safe and sound.

We were standing around while it was pouring rain with two dogs and a lot of heavy luggage when I finally looked at my messages and realized our car rental place wasn't at the airport. We had to call to take a shuttle to get there. So frustrating!

The car they had reserved for me ended up costing almost double than what I reserved it for and then I had to put a $500 deposit down on it as well. Another moment that I was proud of myself for not losing my shit like I may have in the past. I only cussed a little!

They also didn't give me the original car I had reserved. I had to rent a big Dodge Ram truck. Now, I'm used to driving a truck, however the roads here are not like our roads and there is no evidence of road construction around here. Potholes everywhere and very narrow roads!

Needless to say I'm not the greatest driver so this was going to be a joke in itself. Hopefully the truck stays in one piece!

We picked my sister Heidi up from the airport and was on our way when it started to pour down rain again. I rented the truck so I had to be the driver who is terrified of highways especially while it is raining.

I was praying so hard and my sisters didn't even know it. Well, they were probably secretly praying as well!!

We got to our VRBO safe and sound. When we got there I could not get a hold of Jose, our host. We waited for about half an hour before he finally came.

Now, remember I told you it was pouring rain and we had a truck bed which is where we put our luggage, so guess what?? Everything was wet! We spent the first hour or two hanging our clothes to dry because we didn't have a dryer.

Oh well…I wanted an authentic place to stay while experiencing the lifestyle of a Puerto Rican so my request was granted. No bougie hotel or condo for me, it was exactly what I wanted and I loved it!
By now we were starving so off to eat we went! We went to the closest restaurant we could find. It was a seafood restaurant that had crab which is my favorite. People here are in no hurry, we waited an hour and a half for food. My crab was delicious but my sisters did not like their meals that cost $160 for three of us!

After that we went to get groceries to have just a few necessities and that cost $150. Wow, this was an expensive day!

I was starting to wonder if I was going to have to do some hair on the beach while I was here!

We got back to the cottage and just crashed because we were so exhausted.

I slept well and woke up excited to get settled in and ready to explore on this wonderful adventure I was blessed to experience. I'm so happy my sisters came with me now because that first day was challenging and they are truly who I can count on at any given moment!

It is sunny here this morning and I can see the ocean from the porch. How lucky am I? Yesterday is the past and today I'm going to live in the now.

We took Zoie to the beach and she loved it. It was full of happy people and lots of dogs running around. Zoie had the time of her life, however she was very scared of the water. I couldn't believe it because she is a Labradoodle and labs supposedly love the water. I had to take her in like she was my little toddler and try to teach her how to swim. It was hilarious!

The beach is so peaceful and the water is so blue. I could imagine myself living here but let's see how the next twenty six days go.

There are so many sounds of nature here. Birds chirping, cats fighting, dogs barking, and owls hooting. However, the dog that is right behind us could really stop barking anytime that would be great! It barks because it's in a kennel and tied up. That's no way to live.

We feel really bad for it, however it does get annoying when you get woken up by it a lot, not gonna lie. I'm so glad Zoie doesn't bark like that but she is happy and I taught her to use her manners!

The dog situation is really sad here. Everywhere you go there are stray dogs. I can't let Zoie be around them because a lot of them have a skin disease and they do not have a humane society here. When we're on the beach I feel like that bad mom that doesn't let her play with the other kids, makes me sad but I have to protect her.

We went to a restaurant the other night and one was lying on the side of the street dead. Apparently that's a normal thing around here, kind of like a deer on the side of the road in the states.

There are also a lot of wild horses here. One came right up to some grass beside the restaurant where we were eating the other night. My sister Heidi was able to pet it. It would have been fun to have a flash from the past to see her jump on it bareback like we were kids again! I think she was secretly thinking about it.

Something else that's very interesting is that there are a lot of pigeons here and I usually don't like them but they are really pretty birds. Maybe I'm meant to observe them so I can have a better perspective on the behavior of pigeons. One hasn't shit on my head yet so that's a good thing. Life is full of surprises.

As my sisters and I had a great week together exploring, going to the beach, hanging together like we love to do, basically like we were kids again, I was sad to see them go but relieved as well. Sad because I love spending time with them but relieved because I needed this time for myself.

My sisters are my best friends. Growing up, my mom always insisted that we would be close. We did fight a lot but it never took us long to make up. Heidi and I were always the ones to fight, I will humbly admit that I would always beat her up. She was the mouthy one and I had the temper. It's still the same after fifty years.

We had a horrible fight while we were here. We haven't fought like that in a long time. My temper has always been my biggest downfall. I don't like that side of me and I do try my hardest to contain it to the best of my ability now. When I was younger I would just punch people but now I give lots of warning signs before that happens. It's 2023 and you can't just go around hitting people. Even if it's your sister.

We screamed at each other and my sis Lori was very angry at us so we pulled our shit together. We both apologized and moved on with our trip. The WONDERFUL thing that came out of this on my part was that I didn't punch her, also my diaphram felt so much better from yelling so loud!

I suppose we both had been holding in a lot of stress, or something was disturbing us that we needed to release it with someone we felt safe with. We both apologized and perhaps we all three learned something from it as well.

<u>For me, it was my first indication that I was so far out of alignment of being happy. I told myself, "DO BETTER TARA!"</u>

The time had come for my sisters to leave. It was a real vulnerable experience when I drove away from that airport all by myself, just me and my dog Zoie.

I was able to trade the truck in for a car so that made me feel better about driving on a five lane highway, by myself and LITERALLY an ocean away from my reality!

Zoie rode with me so I felt like there was another body in the vehicle. However, she always sits very still right behind me and doesn't say a word, so I'm not sure how much that was going to help me! I silently prayed again and I'm certain if dogs could pray, Zoie was silently praying as well! We got back to the cottage safe and sound. Thank the Lord!
The next day I woke up completely naked, totally vulnerable! I was in complete solitude with just me and my dog. The first full day so I was in complete amazement that this was truly happening!

I started to write about the week I had with my besties. I was trying to relax and get into the realm of solitude.

Then for some reason, that night I started thinking about Pablo. Now, we hadn't seen each other for three months which was about the right amount of time that we would start missing each other.

In the meantime he had texts a few times about wanting his stupid crockpot back that I borrowed from him but for some reason I wouldn't part with it.

I have no idea what that emotion was about because I've never acted like that before, however the answer was always, "no", just my thing I suppose. "I know, do better Tara!"

So, this urge came out of nowhere and I sent him pictures of this beautiful place. He texted me back and it was a friendly conversation. Then I had the urge to call him! WTF? I asked him if he had been thinking about me because I hadn't been thinking of him. I was good with us being apart. He said, "no, but I did have a dream about you last night."
It was an OK conversation but he definitely was his sober, not so vulnerable self. No connection!

I started thinking, "is he subconciously manifesting me, (thinking of me) and is this the reason for this overwhelming urgency to be in contact with him?"

I felt like I was on to something, like the law of attraction was constantly keeping us in connection with each other. Perhaps I wasn't just this needy little desperate woman.

Research time for Tara!

The next day I became a bit more vulnerable and had this weird urge to reach out to my ex-husband Leo's ex-wife. Then Pablo's ex-wife and

ex-girlfriend, you know the one he went back and forth with for several years! Ya, another WTF?
I had no idea what I was thinking.

However, Leo's ex-wife did call me and we had a great conversation. We caught up on life and it was fun!

The other two women have been in contact with me but we still haven't talked vocally at this point of my writing.
I felt as if I needed another woman's validation on my feelings of self worth, the experience I went through with Leo and Pablo, perhaps it was similar for them as well.

I honestly didn't feel like myself. No restraint, complete vulnerability had taken hold of me and I was on this ride that I couldn't get off of.

All I could think of is, "ok, this could possibly be a good piece for my book or I've just completely lost my mind!"

The next several days I was at bay just chillin, writing, hanging with Zoie at the beach having a wonderful time. My friend was struggling with something so I talked her through it while feeling some connection.

It's my nature and when I feel my best is when I'm helping my loved ones through their struggles, rather than if I've been helpful or not.

The next day I decided to go on an adventure with Zoie. We came across this vacant beach which we had no idea because there were cars parked along the road as if there were people around. This little old man even helped me decide where to park. There were men working on that road so I had no idea what to expect. We had to walk along a path to get there. Still no idea where we were going. I wanted to take Zoie somewhere where she could run free, I was hoping this was the place.

At first it was so silent and peaceful that I could hear the ocean waves crashing in. Then we walked up to absolutely no human beings on site. It was a beautiful abandoned beach with a collapsed building, possibly a house at one point with graffiti all over it. I could see houses that had been abandoned on the hillside.

I was videoing it and all of the sudden I saw a homeless person sleeping on the beach beyond some rocks. An overwhelming feeling came over me to exit right away and I heard all the voices in my head of my loved ones saying, "be safe." Zoie kind of acted a little unsettled as well so I listened to my instincts and left right away. It sure was beautiful!

My girls are coming soon so we will definitely go back to visit, take a ball and let Zoie run wild and free!

The same day I was trying to find something to bring me some peace, satisfaction, freedom for Zoie, freedom for myself. I can't really explain it but I was seeking something.

My final destination that day was a pull off the side of the road beach. It was calling me for some reason. There were a few people there so that made me feel more comfortable.

It was beautiful, all the beach views were beautiful here but this one had a swing. I love to swing. It also had some grass. I laid our towel down on the grass and just tried to sit in silence.

I let Zoie off the leash. Now, she has been afraid of the water this whole time so I wasn't worried about the bird being close to the water that was staring at her. It obviously said something she didn't like because about the moment I was in my feel good realm she took off toward the water to chase this bird she had been having a stare down with! No, it wasn't a pigeon! I was so mad at her because it was mucky water. Yuck! Back on the leash for Zoie.

I tried to write but nothing was flowing. So I decided to play some favorite feel good music. All of the sudden I felt so much emotion. I couldn't stop crying and I didnt know why. A voice came in my head telling me that vulnerability is not only to be brave and courageous but to face shame and guilt as well. To forgive myself as well as others.

At that moment, I was playing "Where I Find God" by Larry fleet. I started talking to God, really talking to him more than I ever have in my whole life. I've always believed in God or a higher power, but I have never heard him with such deliverance before. I rarely asked him to help me, I always asked him to help others. I was crying tears of joy. I felt so much comfort.

I then wrote down all the things I felt shameful and guilty for. All the people I wanted to forgive including myself. When I was finished, I ripped it out of my journal, crumpled it up and threw it in the trash can.

I felt so fantastic because I felt and heard GOD!

The next few days I was on top of the world getting so much writing done or just being still for a moment and soaking in this beautiful place that I was so blessed to have manifested into my life story. Watching people from all over the world or simply just playing with my dog who is truly amazing company.

When Zoie was a puppy, she picked me and I'm so grateful I was receptive to that.

So, it was a Friday night I was in bed watching a movie on Netflix when I got a text from Pablo that just said, "ain't always the cowboy."

Now, a couple years ago he sent me that song saying it reminded him of me. It's a beautiful song by Jon Pardi. So I sent him a message back that said, "It's pretty early for you to be drunk already."

Pablo never sent meaningful stuff to me unless he was drinking. We texted back and forth a few times and then he said, "I love you."

<u>For the first time I simply just said, "I know."</u>

He also told me, "he missed me and that he was sorry that he was drunk." I replied, "I know because that's the only time you're vulnerable enough to admit how you feel about me!"

Twelve years is coming up soon on Cinco De Mayo Day so one would think he should have his shit together by now!

Normally I would have said I loved and missed him too but this time I did not. I do still love him and probably always will, however I did not feel like I missed him. My emotions were at bay and I fell asleep.

I woke up the next morning to have missed several texts and two missed calls from him. I responded lightly, with my emotions still at bay and went on with my day.

I had a fishing trip planned with my host, Jose and his son. Jose is a handsome, kind, hospitable man who is going through a divorce. I did not know that when I booked my VRBO as I had spoken to both him and his wife at one point upon arriving here so I was very surprised when I found this out.

My sisters immediately thought for some reason this was going to be a twist to my story and we would end up together from complete destiny. Now, I have to admit he is a remarkable man from what I can see and feel, however I'm not interested in dating a man while going through a divorce. I've been there and done that, IT'S NEVER a good outcome.

We went fishing and had a fantastic time. However, there were moments that I was scared to death because the waves were so gigantic and I felt as if they would suck the boat in with one gulp! I just secretly prayed to God, relaxed and enjoyed the ride.

That same morning before my fishing trip I had another urge to reach out to my friend that I had fallen out with and hadn't spoken to for well over a year.

I had been very hurt by her words and actions towards me and always felt as if she had higher expectations of me than she did of her own self. I love her dearly but I started to not like the person she had become.

She had suffered from a lot of grief in her life and I was always there for her through those times, however she could not realize the pain she was projecting onto her loved ones that were still here on earth. I felt as if nothing I did was enough anymore and that I always had to understand her but she couldn't or just simply didn't want to understand me. We had just grown apart.

The day before I had received a notification that she was following me on Tic Tok. At first I was annoyed by it but then I realized why she was doing it, she was worried about me.

Then a little voice popped in my head saying, "it's time to reach out Tara."

I was feeling very vulnerable and not sure how she would respond. I sent her a heartfelt message assuring her I was fine and that I would like to get together and talk when I get home.

It took her forever to respond and when she did it was very vague, not mean, but not really what I had hoped for as well. Perhaps I overthink things especially when I'm being vulnerable.

Fearful of rejection is a horrible state of mind.

We text back and forth for a bit and it was a good feeling. Perhaps a great step in the right direction to get us back on track. Not only for the two of us but for the big circle of people in our lives that have always loved us both.

After the fishing trip I showered and decided to get all dolled up to get a bite to eat and take Zoie for a walk to this place by the beach that has my new favorite drink.

I ran into my Canadian couple along the way who was staying at the top level of my beach cottage. They were sitting on the bench watching the sunset, I told them I'd come back to join them.

As I was walking back I felt as if they saw me coming and got up and left. I was so disappointed.

They were a very nice couple and always friendly but I felt as if they were possibly avoiding my company at times and I didnt understand why. I wasn't used to that because I'm always making friends and I feel as if people normally enjoy my company.

I sat down on the bench, staring out at the ocean feeling very alone with my thoughts. I started to become so overwhelmed with emotions. I was spiraling fast, like I was ready to have a complete meltdown! I started to cry and a little voice came to me again that said "reach out Tara."
I decided to call my friend Karen who is the person in my life who completely understands what vulnerability means and what it feels like. I also

knew she wouldn't freak out by worrying about me and want to get on the first plane out to save me!

She didn't answer! She texted me and said she was in her clinic but that she would call me back in an hour. I said, "I need you NOW but that I was ok." She knew that wasn't like me, so she immediately went to the break room and called me back.

I told her all the events that had happened so she helped me put everything back into perspective. Perhaps I was having a vulnerability overload which caused me to have a meltdown.

I felt better so I went back to the cottage and had a drink with Jose along with a good conversation. He was going through a lot of emotions with his divorce so I just listened, offered some support and that made my day end well.

The next day it came to me that the reason the couple upstairs made me feel like they were avoiding me was because that was their universal purpose that was manifested by me.

When I planned this trip I wanted to be in solitude without having to entertain anyone or be of purpose for anyone else but myself, my writing and my dog. I asked to feel safe and comfortable in knowing someone would be there for me if I should have any issues. After that I never felt that rejection again. I had put myself back into alignment with that emotion.

They are a lovely couple that make me smile when I see them and perhaps knowing why they are here without them even being aware of it.

<u>I totally manifested them!</u>

They were here when I got here and are staying here until three days after I leave. Oh and by the way… they own a printing company as well and print books for a publishing company in Quebec!

"God is good!"

The next day I needed a free day. Zoie and I went exploring again and this time we found a perfect beach. She got to play with other dogs and I just enjoyed myself.

I met a couple from Michigan so it was nice having a conversation with someone who spoke perfect English. That was a bit of a struggle for me because I have comprehension hearing loss which makes it difficult to understand those who speak broken English.

When I got back to the cottage for some reason I started feeling like my book was going to be a disaster and that I shouldn't reveal so much of my personal experiences for fear of judgment and possible hurt feelings. I thought, "do people even care what I have to say"? I was spiraling fast and felt like I was ready to have another complete meltdown! I thought about deleting my book completely!

This time I didn't hear a voice but I did smell something that was familiar… My dad always used a Zippo lighter and I loved the smell of it. I would always buy him a new one for Christmas or his Birthday.

Typically when I was needing to feel his presence he would always show me he was there through dandelions in the strangest places. Dandelions were his favorite flower but Puerto Rico didn't have them. It was right then that I realized it was him letting me know he was with me.

They say angles will let you know they are there through smell as well as visual signs. You just have to believe and be receptive to it. I had smelled it a couple other times prior to that night but I didn't put that much thought into it. I was struggling with exploiting so much family baggage because that's not my MO, however there are things people do that they need to be accountable for. I also couldn't leave certain things out if I were going to tell the story of my life.

I felt as if he was giving me his blessing.

I then noticed a book that my sister left here, a book that I had let her borrow, "SUPER ATTRACTOR" by Gabrielle Bernstein. I decided to read it.

The thing is, I couldn't remember if i had read it before but she was making perfect sense to me now! I was open and allowed her words to flow to me as if we were having a real conversation. I was present. I spent the next day reading as if it were my bible.

For several days after that I continued to write and read. When I would get stuck I would just "be" in the moment and have a playdate with Zoie. I started to just have fun and stop putting so much pressure on myself. I became truly happy. I felt joy and peace within me. I felt "alive" for the first time in my life.

It was two days before my daughters were coming to visit for a week. It was going to be our first vacation with just the three of us. I was so excited for them to be coming!

That morning I had a great conversation with my sis Lori. I was talking to her about her job and the words were just flowing out of my mouth so easily about that she was the eagle and was to be leading the ducks to a higher altitude.

She was on a short term administration job at the time and was having a bit of a struggle with some issues there. I felt as if I helped her with just that short yet uncomplicated statement. How to get people back into alignment when you're a leader.

It was at that moment I found my strategy with another purpose for me writing this book and possibly another one. To better understand the theory of manifesting and the law of attraction. It felt amazing and made me feel on top of the world.

It's time for me to get ready to go pick up my girls so I have to stop writing for just a bit. I'll explain later until then, "Just remember…. **EAGLES SOAR, DUCKS QUACK, PIGEONS SHIT!"**

Good morning, I'm back and picking my girls up was amazing. I had a few close calls on the highway and I'm certain that Zoie and my girls were silently praying again because I know I was several times!

I had never been more excited to see my baby girls since the day that I was blessed to birth them. I know that through the years I had been out of alignment with them at times as well so this was my time to just enjoy every minute with them. There is nothing that brings me more joy than to spend precious time with my beautiful daughters.

Our family had something very tragic happen at one point that tore us apart for over a year. I wish to leave this part out because I don't want or need to revisit it.

I will tell you that you have to be careful with your children when they enter the dating age and always keep the communication open. When you are divorced parents, always stand strong together for what's best for your children, not just what could possibly be best for you.

We all got through it thankfully and I have forgiven myself for my part and asked God to heal us all from it.

Raising children, especially being single, is one of the toughest, most humbling yet rewarding jobs you can have!

I wanted this time for my girls to get back to feeling that sibling love for eachother and to realize no matter how different they are they will always be connected….

A true soulful best friend, someone you can always count on!

I feel like this is my time now to enjoy them. To be able to support, guide and encourage them, that it is possible to live your best life. I could finally lead by example with ease and grace. It's going to be a great week!

It was a fantastic week. We went to Old San Juan, wow that was beautiful! We went to a beautiful, somewhat secluded beach and just relaxed and let Zoie be free to play. We went shopping and ate at fantastic restaurants all week.

The absolute best day was riding horses on the beach. My Canadian friends joined us as well and we had a blast. The girls loved every minute of it and I couldn't stop smiling and feeling so blessed. My horse's name was destiny, imagine that!

I was so amazed when we rode past that abandoned beach that I wanted to explore. I was so happy to be able to see it again. It was on my to do list when the girls got here but we hadn't made it there yet so that was completely amazing! I feel as if my girls were so mesmerized by the beauty that was all around them.

I'm not going to sugarcoat it though as there were some moments that I had to use a new technique that I learned from Gabrielle. It is when someone you love triggers your emotions and you feel like a confrontation is brewing, so you just visualize the happiest moment you had with them. Well lets just say, I had to rebirth them both a few times!

It's funny that you go from being a child, to a parent, back to a child again! I just surrendered to not knowing how or what to do the right way anymore and let them take care of me! "It really worked Gabrielle, Thank you." I didn't have to drive or cook the whole time. Yay!

I feel as if I did a good job raising my girls. I wasn't perfect by any means, and it wasn't easy to deal with my own life traumas while raising them, however I'm extremely proud of the beautiful women they turned out to be.

I want them to enjoy their journey and learn lessons to help them grow just as I have. That true success in life is feeling peace and happiness within themselves beyond anything else.

I will always be here for them with my love, support and guidance if they need me. I will not interfere or cause havoc over the way I think they should be and just appreciate them for who they aspire to be.

I will always remind them of the beauty of this world and that they will always have choices and the ability to change them no matter how difficult things may seem.

I hope that they will always be humble and kind.

Full of gratitude and generosity.

And most of all…to know that they will always be loved by me.

I Woke up Naked - Tara Flaherty

"Don't worry that your children never listen to you; Worry that they are always watching you."

-Robert Fulghum-

This amazing trip made me well aware that I needed to go there not just to write my book but perhaps to heal from the many challenges, heartbreaks, and disappointments I had been suppressing for most of my life.

I felt peace within me while taking this time for myself and was ready to squash any low self worth issues I may have been feeling towards myself.

<u>I am a beautiful soul of God and must always remind myself of that!</u>

"When you change the way you see things, The things you see will change."
-Wayne Dyer-

Discovery of my journey

I feel like if we really pay attention to our signs it can be magical. I believe everything happens for a reason, to truly believe and feel it to be true, that is where the peace and joy lies.

While I was in Puerto Rico my signs led me to a powerful message with the help of reading Gabrielle Bernstein's book "SUPER ATTRACTOR."

The way we feel is the most important aspect in attracting everything we want for our lives.

Our emotions and how we react to them are an indicator to what vibrational altitude (emotional level) we are on.

I've always used the bird method to compare what type of person we are being.

Soar like an eagle, don't quack like a duck and definitely don't shit like a pigeon.

Who are you? What is your perception of this beautiful world? Are you an eagle, duck or a pigeon?

Eagle
The eagle soars through life gracefully. They are mysterious and usually enjoy their own company. They take risks as they fly to the highest altitude without being intimidated by others. They come in for their prey fiercely and know exactly what they need to survive. Strongest and king or queen of the birds. An eagle is a symbol of beauty, bravery, courage, honor, pride, determination and grace.

Duck
The duck quacks and waddles. They usually like to hang with other ducks to see how loud they can quack together. They are smart and pretty but can be very picky on who they let hang with their flock. They are very emotional and typically are very intimidated by their prey. They like to flock together and don't like to take risks.

Pigeon
The pigeon poops five times per hour. In retrospect they shit all over everything and everybody. They are a pest plain and simple. However they are beautiful and smart and they stay in a pack and will wait for the right moment to swoop in and take what you have. There are usually a few leaders who appear to be a little different that bully others for fear they will miss out on something they think they need more than others.

I have discovered that they are all beautiful birds created from GOD (gift of diversity). There is definitely a difference in how they ascend in this world.

<u>A distinct observation we should all be aware of and possibly compare to the vibrational altitude (emotional level) we are on.</u>

I never really had any meaningful interactions with pigeons except for when I was a child, they lived in our barn and shit all over everything and possibly our heads a time or two! I started comparing mean people to pigeons because I had been feeling hurt recently by people I loved dearly. I felt as if they were being shitty pigeons.

I finally was able to really observe pigeons on a more meaningful level in Puerto Rico. They were all around me while I was sitting on the beach. I started to notice how beautiful they were.

So one day I threw a bunch of crackers out and they came flocking out of nowhere towards me! It was like they were starving, desperate and fearful that there wasn't going to be enough to share. Then a few bullies kept messing with a few of them like they didn't deserve anything.

I suddenly realized they were just on a lower vibration, that even though they were perhaps shitty birds they were also beautiful birds created from god. Desperate, fearful and hateful makes everyone and everything vibrate at a lower level.

I was definitely on to something with my bird analogy. How you feel and your actions allow you to recognize what vibration you are on. The eagle vibration is the highest. That is when you are happy and feel at peace to live your best life.

I'm using a brilliant mentor's emotional guide to make you aware of what level of emotions you are going through. I also added the separation of the Three levels comparative to the birds.

The next page is another brilliant mentor's guide to help you change your vibration (emotion) to bring you back to a higher level.

<u>I feel as if PEACE is the highest vibration to God!</u>

Emotional guidance scale - Abraham Hicks-

EAGLE= highest vibration
1. Joy/Appreciation/Empowered/Freedom/Love
2. Passion
3. Enthusiasm /Eagerness/Happiness
4. Positive Expectation/Belief
5. Optimism
6. Hopefulness
7. Contentment

DUCK= idle vibration
8. Boredom
9. Pessimism
10. Frustration/Irritation/Impatience
11. Overwhelment
12. Disappointment
13. Doubt
14. Worry

PIGEON= lowest vibration
15. Blame
16. Discouragement
17. Anger
18. Revenge
19. Hatred/Rage
20. Jealousy
21. Insecurity/Guilt/Unworthiness
22. Fear/Grief/Desperation/Despair/Powerlessness

Choose again method- Gabrielle Bernstein-

1. Notice the fear.

Notice when your fearful thoughts start sabotaging your positive flow, and ask yourself, "how do I feel right now?" Let yourself feel whatever is coming up for you.

2. Forgive the thought.

Forgive yourself for fearing the good feelings. Say out loud or silently, "I forgive this thought and I choose to believe in love instead." Then celebrate your desire to shift back to feeling good!

3. Choose again.

Answer this question, "what is the best feeling-thought I can find right now?" Then thank the universe for guiding you toward that thought.

We can change our thoughts at any given moment.

<u>**Our thoughts control our emotions which then control our actions!**</u>

I would like to write another book, most likely in Puerto Rico, explaining this theory in more detail on how to manifest and maintain your vibration while flying to the highest altitude.That's where miracles happen.

It has been two months since I've been back from Puerto Rico and I had just finished my book. I sent it off to be edited by a friend of mine's mother who used to be an English professor. Boy was I nervous! English used to be my best subject, however writing a book at fifty one can really make you grateful for technology and spell check!

I also printed a copy for my mom. I wanted to make sure she was ok with my memories as there were some personal things in it about our lives. It meant a lot to me to have her approval. That made me extremely nervous! To my surprise and hers as well, she liked it. That made me feel so good.

My mom is complimentary, however she has always made us work for what we had....including our talents! We were taught to be gracious, not egotistical!

Perhaps you could always become better with a little more effort.

She said it was really good but felt it needed a little more detail. I knew that it did but I kept getting writer's block and just wanted to be done. She inspired me to keep going so once again I became vulnerable….

The farm that I grew up on as a child with both my parents was up for auction a couple years ago. It looked a lot like it did when we bought it many years ago because apparently the people didn't take care of it for whatever reason.

The company named Hochstetler bought it, tore the old farmhouse down and built a beautiful 1.9 million dollar log home on it. It's breathtaking and I would love to manifest it into my reality.

However, I became fearless and called the number of the company and asked if I could go sit on the porch to soak up some memories from the property to finish my book. The lady was so nice and said she didn't think it was a problem but that she would have to ask the owner.

A few days later my phone rang and I was talking to the big guy. The owner of the 1.9 million dollar house that was built on the land that I grew up on. He was very interested in my story so he said I could go there anytime and that he would be very interested in reading my book. I told him that I was going to sell over one hundred and fifty thousand copies of my book so that I could buy his house.

I could have it for a writers retreat, my retreat or simply for my family retreat as it is where we all have wonderful memories.

Manifesting in the works!

I went to the property and sat on the porch a couple times. It was so peaceful. I felt as if it were my home already. I didn't get a lot of writing done but I did get a lot of thinking done and it brought back so many beautiful memories that I have longed for my whole life. Perhaps the peace I've been searching for since we moved from there many years ago. I felt as if I were finally home again where I belong.

I loved to climb trees as a child and one time I climbed to the top of this huge pine tree and couldn't get down. I kept yelling for help and finally my mom and dad heard me so my dad had to climb up to rescue me. Those pine trees are still there, bigger than ever as I can see them from this magnificent million dollar porch. I doubt I could climb a tree that big again but it would be fun to try!

"No dream is too big."

I Woke up Naked - Tara Flaherty

"What you think you become.
What you feel you attract.
What you imagine you create."

<u>Keep your thoughts positive, because your thoughts become your words. Keep your words positive because your behaviors become your habits. Keep your habits positive, because your habits become your values. Keep your values positive, because your values become your destiny.</u>
-Gandhi-

As for me……. I climbed that tree!

As for Pablo….. Well after I got back from Puerto Rico he contacted me to let me know his son was moving to Indiana the next morning and he knew that I would most likely want to see him. So I went because I just love his boys. I tried to remain strong and not desire him like I always have. It worked for a little while but he didn't like the word "NO" so he continued to try with me.

I found myself desiring him more and more as it had been almost four months since I slept with him.

Everytime I have sex with him it feels like a fifty-first date! When he touches me I don't want him to stop! My soul is completely connected to him. Even if we are just laying in bed going to sleep, I have to feel him. His skin feels so soft up against mine and I feel as if we are meant to become one beautiful couple so in love.

He always tells me I have spaghetti legs because I have to have them wrapped around him so tight. I feel like a leach but I never want to let go.

The whole F###ING process started over again!

This time I know he loves me because he kept professing that to me but I also know in my heart that he was most likely not going to be any different!

I just enjoyed our time, did my own thing with my friends, and focused on my salon while wrapping up my book.

He did seem different this time, we talked a lot about our feelings and that if he were going to commit to anyone that it would be me. He even told my nephew that he was going to be his uncle someday!

I tried to believe him but I also had to realize he was most likely just drunk talking with that statement because one never knows when it came to Pablo. He would always promise everyone the world while he was drunk and then when he was sober it became a different story!

Everything seemed to be going good until...

We were having a party for some friends. A friend that I met years ago through Pablo was coming over that I had suspected something sexual happened between them before we met. I just had that feeling because of how flirtatious they were with each other. Everyone else did as well but they always denied it.

Through the years I finally just let it go and didn't worry about it any longer. She and I became good friends. She always had extreme relationship issues so I always tried to comfort her while listening to all the dysfunction.

A few months prior, she asked if I minded if she would go to dinner with Pablo because she really needed his friendship with something she was going through. I told her I didn't mind at all as I thought that would be good for her.

Weeks went by and I had a trip planned to go to Nashville with some girlfriends. While I was there Pablo was being kind of shitty with me but I just realized he would always be that way when I was away with my friends. When I got home he was still distant so I just did my own thing.

I reached out to my friend to see if they ever went to dinner. She was very vague and said, "yes but couldn't remember when". I said, "wow, that's weird because you're not even fifty yet"! She spilled it and said they went to dinner and to the movies while I was in Nashville. That was cool but I still had an uneasy feeling about it.

The day came for the party and I was having a terrible day. Rushing to try to get everything accomplished before the party. That morning I went to see my aunt who was dying of cancer. That was extremely hard as it was my dads youngest sister and I loved her so much.

My emotions were very unsettled for my day to begin with.

I went to the store in a rush and got back to Pablo's to cook for everyone so that they could have a nice birthday party.

We all started drinking and I saw my friend reach over and softly rub Pablo's back. Not just a pat on the back but a sensual rub that could possibly give you a tingle! I didn't want to make a scene so I let it go and just told myself to keep my eyes open.

I ended up not eating anything all night and the alcohol took over! Apparently I got upset and "temperamental tara " came out, perhaps because my instincts were correct. I didn't punch anyone but I became feisty!

I found out from a few guests that were there that they were kissing and dancing with each other, he was trying to rub her in inappropriate places and even mysteriously came up missing for quite some time upstairs while the rest of us were in the basement. I'm pretty sure, "Temperamental Tara" may have come out of retirement if I would have caught them doing something inappropriate.

However, my friend can just thank the Lord, while she's in church, that I didn't! I'm certain that the farm girl may be still in me just a little! Just sayin!

They both denied it, however I feel as if they can't hide the deceit any longer. I was so deeply hurt. I left that next morning and told Pablo I wouldn't be back. I didn't feel mad, I just felt sad that they both could do that to me.

I also felt a sense of relief this time, perhaps that I was finally done being degraded for good. I was able to walk away as a good person, still full of love not lies!

I love him but he will always be searching for some kind of thrill of a chase or deceit instead of love and stability. Same for my friend!

<u>Apparently, guilt and shame must not be something they feel for others until it's too late.</u>

I tried to explain my pain to both of them a few days later because I couldn't get it out of my mind. It ended up hurting me so deeply, however I feel they do not feel anything on that level, nor would they admit to doing anything wrong.

I honestly feel as if I expected this from Pablo and that perhaps it was the betrayal of my friend that hurt the most. She knew how much I loved him.

My friend finally clarified that, "yes", Pablo tried to make the moves on her and that she declined and tried to avoid the situation for fear of making a scene. However, I don't feel as if rubbing someone's back in a sensual manner is an indication of avoidance, it's more like an open invitation to pursue!

"To the depth of my despair, the hole in my heart yearns for the love that I so desire, however I can't seek that from a broken soul without him willing to heal his own heart."

I knew this during my healing process while I was in Puerto Rico, however I was willing to become vulnerable to Pablo one last time.

On the contrary, had I not, then perhaps I would have always wondered if the love he professed to me after I got back was real.

My conclusion is that it is not sustainable, never has been nor will be until he admits to himself that he needs some professional help with the dysfunction that lies within him from his past traumas.

I don't regret the past twelve years I've spent with Pablo as I have many wonderful memories and he is a special person to me.

We don't have to hate someone that we love just because things didn't work out in our favor.

There is a reason I was with him for so long and only God knows why. He is the only one who is allowed to judge our relationship and the journey we went on together!

However, I've grown from this chapter of my life and I'm ready and willing to end it gracefully.

As my momma always tells me, "this too shall pass!"

<u>I will no longer be a maybe or a second choice. I'm not an option when it's convenient. I'm definitely not a, "wait and see", I am an absolute YES!</u>

I've learned to love myself unconditionally and no longer feel like a victim to the feeling of low self worth. The only person that holds us captive to that is our own self!

I'm sorry to my readers that the story of Pablo was not a good fairytale ending. I do know that everything happens for a reason and that sometimes no matter how nice, kind, caring or loving you are, it just isn't going to be enough for some people.

The lessons I have learned from this are valuable and I do know that it's not just a piece of paper from the court that will make you keep trying when you love someone with your whole heart!

"I want a man that loves, values, respects and adores me. Someone who admires me for my independence and aspirations and is not intimidated by that."

A man that will be proud of me for caring about others and will trust me to have fun with my friends as he is having fun in life as well.

Definitely a man that is proud of me for being brave enough to be the first one on the dance floor and he will know that it's just simply because **I LOVE** to dance!

A man that is confident with himself and looks at life in a positive aspect and allows me to be my own individual.

A man that also loves, values and respects himself as well. There is nothing that I would desire more than that of a resilient man!

Women have to continue to inspire each other while going through this aging process in life. We should empower one another.

<u>**Never EVER should we prey on another woman's man!**</u>

This could be shameful and totally driven from insecurities, jealousy, manipulation, desperate need of attention or perhaps low self worth. Which could make you vibrate at the pigeon level.

We also have to remember that our wrinkles are just wise lines, gray hair can be covered and that everything we face just makes us stronger. We are still beautiful, nurturing souls that bring life to this amazing world!

"When you become a strong, independent person and you live your life as a beautiful individual, a partner becomes a bonus to it, not a necessity."

-Tara Flaherty-

And as for Zoie... she's glad this book is finally finished! She wants to play and get my undivided attention.

She also can't wait to go back to Puerto Rico!

As for the beautiful ladies in my life……
My mom still lives in Ohio with my bonus dad Doug of thirty years and they are happy and healthy.

Heidi lives in Tennessee engaged to a wonderful man living her best life. She had three beautiful children.

Lori lives in Ohio married to a wonderful man as well living her dream job as an Administrator of a nursing home. She had two beautiful children.

All is well….

Success

To laugh often and much, to win the respect of intelligent people and the affection of children.

To earn the appreciation of honest critics and Endure the betrayal of false friends.

To appreciate beauty, to find the best in others, to leave the world a bit better, whether by a healthy child, a garden patch, or a redeemed social condition.

To know even one life has breathed easier because you have lived.

That is to have succeeded.

-Ralph Waldo Emerson-

Real World

Open your eyes to the real world
To see what you could be
Don't be trapped inside
Get out and set yourself free.
Take your time, be choosey
Don't get tied down,
Realize the good you have
Always smile, don't frown.
Happiness is special
In life as you go,
Whenever you get lost
Let your loved ones know.
Don't depend on someone
To do the things you should,
Never let your loved ones down
If you know they never would.
Have respect for one another
And show that you care,
Your in the real world so
Always have love to spare.

- Tara Flaherty -

What if life wasn't full of rainbows and positivity?

Where would we all be?
Rainbows are real!
Positivity is a beautiful mindset.
Why can't this be a true state of mind?
Why does misery love company?
Soar like an eagle, is it a peaceful state or confined state like being a duck and not able to fly to the highest altitude?
Why do we limit ourselves?
Should life be full of fear with all the unknown limitations we put on ourselves and others?
Should we not think out of the box?
I think not!
I love it when I see a rainbow or a happy person spreading words of positivity.
Why can't that be what we all aspire for in this life?
Why do we hold on to negative beliefs to feel safe?

"I'm looking for the rainbow and I want to soar with the eagles to see the colorful life that God intended for our world to be."

-Tara Flaherty-

Juot one more thing….to be continued

Acknowledgments

Thank you to my family for all your support and confidence in me while I was dedicating my time from start to the completion of this book. I'm certain that I was a PITA a time or two.

Thank you to my momma for not letting me sell my house during this process as it is my beautiful sanctuary!

I feel you have taught us girls to be resilient, independent and gracious women. You have always reminded us to be good to life and life will be good to you.

Your strength can be conflicting to us at times, however it has molded us into the women we are today. "I'm so proud to have you for my mother, I love you."

Writing a book about your life isn't easy as you go through a tremendous amount of emotions upon remembrance and reflection. It's a very humbling yet rewarding experience.

Thank you to my friends and clients for all your encouraging words and patience through this amazing experience. I know I can always count on you all to be my cheerleader even if I want to go away for a month while your hair may need me so much more.

Thank you Tracy for being the critiquer for my book while you were recovering from your surgery. You kept me motivated and inspired that I could truly help people. I appreciate you in so many ways.

Thank you Sabine and Chadi for giving me this opportunity with your printing company, Katasoho Design & Print, as well as keeping me inspired.

It was so amazing to meet you in Puerto Rico and I'm looking forward to making it a yearly reunion.

Most of all, thank you God for the amazing strength and guidance you give me to live my best life. I am blessed with your grace.

Testimonials

My youngest little go-getter, positive thinking daughter has worked very hard to share some of her inspirational stories with all of you. Hopefully it will help some folks to see their future in a new light by just changing their view about life!

Alice Sanz- mother

"Like a rainbow after a storm or a soft light from afar guiding you home, Tara Sue Flaherty's brightness shines from within and has always been there: daughter, sister, friend to lighten this sometimes dim world we live in!"

Lori Marsh-Lykins- sister

Tara Sue Flaherty's lifelong dream to write an inspirational book is finally coming true after so much hard work. I am very proud of my little sister and hope it will be a huge success!

Heidi Morrison- sister

"Like a dandelion in the grass, my mom brings light to the openness of life."

She encourages me to strive to become my best self, always. I can count on her on my good, bad and ugly days as she never lets me down.

I'm so proud of the woman she is, as I strive to be as driven and independent as she is.

Katelin Thompson-Daughter

I witnessed the love between Tara and Pablo for years. What a beautiful connection they had when they were together!

Sometimes love doesn't present itself all nice and pretty, "sometimes it's just too complicated".

I think they both gave it all they were capable of giving. Unfortunately, sometimes a person's best just isn't enough.

Karen Clifton- Friend

Tara is one of those people that naturally draws people to her, with her love for life and caring heart. Her strong and independent personality allows her to take on any challenge she faces as an opportunity to learn and grow.

She genuinely makes people feel special and important and loves to inspire others.

I'm lucky to have called her a friend my entire life and always look forward to my tara-therapy sessions. We share and vent, laugh and cry, while she makes me look and feel beautiful. I always leave feeling uplifted.

Chris Stanger- Lifelong friend/client (Kindergarten)

I met Tara back in 1991 when she became my stylist. Through the years I have learned alot about her as a person as she became a dear friend to me.

Tara has been able to pursue her dreams while maintaining persistence as it is possibly one of her greatest attributes. She understands herself and does not allow others to criticize her for deciding who she is and what she is meant to accomplish for her own life.

She has an inner need to understand her place and purpose in God's world. She understands what she is meant to do and more importantly why.

Tara believes God (Gift of Diversity) has created us all to be beautiful, different and unique for a reason.

Sandra Blevins- Lifelong client/friend

I have known Tara for many years. Not only is she a fantastic hairstylist, her creativity is beyond awesome. I have quite a few of her art pieces in my home that are absolutely beautiful!

Now she has become an author, when she sets her mind on something she goes after it. There is nothing she can't do.

If Tara has any faults at all it is that she puts everyone else first before herself.

I have learned so much from her during my monthly visits, I truly love her and consider her a dear friend of mine.

Joey Caudill- Client/friend

I've never met anyone that could always find the good in everyone and everything even when there wasn't…

She has always been an inspiration to me watching her go through lots of hard life challenges, however she is always Concord no matter what!

She has always found a way to be a positive person and get through what she had to!

Charlie- friend

Tara has been an amazing inspiration to us to always be positive and thankful among other things in our daily lives.

Through many years together, once a month, listening to her encouragement we have learned how to manifest our business so we can continue to be passionate and creative to help make it a success!

Rob & Elizabeth Lynn- clients/friends

I have known Tara for twenty three years now. I was privileged to read her book and give her my input while I was recovering from surgery.

Tara is a very independent woman and that is what impressed me!

Even though I'm eleven years older than her I wanted to be her in my new adult life. I met Tara after a nasty divorce at age forty, shortly after she opened her first Salon. She gave me my new look so I could feel better about myself and she succeeded.

After having the privilege to read her book it has brought back so many memories of what my friend has gone through and how amazing she is to look at the world in her own way.

She is a beautiful strong woman and I am very proud to be one of her many friends!

Tracey L. Harrington- client/friend

About the Author

Tara Flaherty grew up on a farm near the small town of Perrysville, Ohio. She became an entrepreneur by opening her own beauty salon as a single mother at the young age of 24.

She wants to express to the world how many times she has woken up naked feeling very vulnerable to the many changes and challenges she has gone through.

She hopes to inspire you to put the past behind you, live in the now and be hopeful of your future. To know that you are in complete control of your own thoughts and you can change them at any given moment.

Adversity builds strength and allows you to persevere to become the best leader of your own life.

"To live successfully is not expecting perfection, it is finding peace with the life you are living."

Made in the USA
Middletown, DE
26 September 2023